THE EXAMINED LIFE

First edition

ISBN 978-0-9921071-0-9

Printed in Canada

Design: Mike Berson
Photo of author: Marc Muri

THE EXAMINED LIFE

BY
BRAM
LEVINSON

To Sharif Shukr, who was
the first person to ever tell me that
if I wrote a book, he'd buy it.

To Peter McNaughton, who bought
me a pen decades ago and
ordered me to start using it.

To Adriana Palanca, who co-edited
this book and commiserated with me
whenever I lost my way.

To Vanessa Muri, who also co-edited
this book and brought
her royal twinness to the work.

Thank you.

To my teachers:
Joan Ruvinsky, Jennifer Maagendans,
Mark Darby, and Richard Miller.

I am blessed to have you
as guides along my journey.

To Stephane,
without whom,
I'd be nothing.

It is never late to ask yourself

"Am I ready to change my life,
am I ready to change myself?"

However old we are,
whatever we went through,
it is always possible to reborn.

If each day is a copy of
the last one, what a pity!

Every breath is a chance to reborn.
But to reborn into a new life,
you have to die before dying.

Shams Tabrizi

CONTENTS

INTRODUCTION

How do you feel about your life up to this point? Are you getting somewhere, closer to where you want to be, or are you just maintaining, staying alive, going through the motions? What matters to you? What's your take on spirituality? What do you believe in? Are your beliefs those that have been handed over to you by others? What about happiness? Are you happy? Is happiness something that you strive to incorporate into your life at every possible moment, or is it something that once achieved, feels less satisfying and freeing than you expected? Do you even know where to look for it?

There are countless questions that we could and should be asking ourselves throughout our lives. As one who continues to seek answers to countless questions, I also know that the process of searching can be overwhelmingly demanding and frighteningly time-consuming. Millions of people ask themselves questions every day that could lead them to a higher state of being, but abruptly stop the process when the self-reflection brings them to a place of challenge, self-confrontation and fear. This book, in fact, my entire career, is about making that process easier, more user-friendly. It's about helping people look at life differently and knowing where to start in the examination of who we are, why we're here, how we relate to each other, and how to live a life steeped in happiness, peace, strength, clarity, and hope. This is not about giving you concrete answers or solutions, but rather pointing you in the right direction so you know where to look. It's about providing insight and information that you may not already have been exposed to.

This project started out as a workshop, one given to yoga students at studios and conferences around North America to serve as a starting point or ongoing tool for their personal development. My inherently inquisitive nature led me to yoga relatively early on in my life when my own personal development started to demand my attention, and it was through my yoga studies and teacher training that I found so many answers to the existential questions I found myself reflecting upon in my daily meanderings. As typically happens, those answers led to more questions as I began to understand the limitless boundaries within which we live, and so this book helps keep seekers on the right path to discovering what they're searching for.

Much of the insight in this book stems from personal reflections based on my experience, but much of it also stems from the yoga teachings, most obviously the *Yoga Sutras of Patanjali*, the *Bhagavad Gita*, and the tales from Hindu mythology. As any teacher with an ounce of good sense will tell you, the elements that *The Examined Life* is comprised of don't start and end with me. I have learned through my observations, from my teachers, and by ceaselessly challenging norms and asking questions. My interpretation is offered, absolutely, but to coin a phrase I've always been fond of, *I'm not making the news, I'm just reporting it.* What's being reported will resonate with everyone, regardless of whether or not they practice yoga.

I still give *The Examined Life* workshop and find that it grows as I do, expanding to include morsels of insight and thought-provoking concepts that can only appear through life's endless lessons and their practical application. I find that when applied, these concepts have brought me closer to a place of truth and clarity. There have been moments when I didn't want to take my own advice, when I had to hear it from those around me who were familiar with my teachings and were forced to relay them back to me. But ultimately, I always found my way back to them, facing my own fears and apprehensions, and battling through them. It is because I have experienced these shifts in perception and clarity that I feel compelled to share what I've learned, originally through my classes and the workshop, and now through this book.

What *The Examined Life* essentially strives to be is a call to the present moment. It is about letting go of what lies in the past, understanding that the more we dwell on what has already happened, the more we end up dragging the past into the future, over and over, until we have exhausted ourselves. It is about shifting from a life spent immersed in mediocrity to one lived beyond all hopes and expectations. It is about understanding that mediocrity is the most effective camouflage for the uncertain, and that those unable to identify what's not quite right in their lives, who simply exist day-to-day with no real direction or passion, have become masters of uncertainty, begging for life to pull them out of their slump. It is about letting ourselves off the hook for what we've been beating ourselves up over, understanding that the punishment has already happened. What lays in wait is never as bad as the suffering we inflict on ourselves when we dwell on the past. It is about letting go of our semblance of control over the future, knowing that we don't really have control over most of it. It is a system of tools that allows us to ask ourselves why we're alive on earth at this present moment in time, how we have lived our lives up to this point, and how we want to live the rest of the time that we are afforded. It is a detailed reminder that happiness is not defined by what you have or want, but rather by how you think. It not only serves as a touchstone for those going through massive upheavals in their lives, but also for those who find themselves unable to find happiness despite having followed the generally accepted protocols. It also offers direction for those who, like me, simply feel that there's much more to life than the obvious.

Many people will read this collection of thoughts and find its contents straightforward and obvious. Others might find real insight into who they have been, or wish to be. And, hopefully, others might find the subject matter revolutionary, a practical collection of tools that when put to the test serve to bring about positive change. Regardless of how and if it affects you, I believe that this book has found its way to you for a reason. I urge you to never accept anything blindly or at face-value, including the words in this book. After you've read a chapter, put the book down and reflect on what you've read and what sensations, emotions, thoughts or reactions the subject matter has elicited. Take notes. Meditate on it all. Take everything in and take your time. Absorb what speaks to you, and then practically apply it to your lives. See if it changes anything.

CHANGING THE WAY YOU THINK

What's your take on destiny versus free will? Have you come to the realization that despite having done everything you thought would bring you happiness, it's still proving to be elusive?

Many people believe that life ends up being one of two things:

1. a series of decisions that we make because it's expected of us, or
2. a series of opportunities that gravitate towards us and which we pursue.

A series of decisions that we make because it's expected of us... by our families, our friends, our workmates, society, etc... Hundreds of millions of people do what is expected of them in matters of the heart, the wallet, the workplace, and the family. Following the proper channels of education, which lead us to the proper career that pays the proper salary, which allows us to buy the proper house, car, television, clothes, etc... Becoming romantically involved with the proper person who represents the proper family stemming from a lineage good enough to align with one's own. Spending time with people who reflect back to us what we'd like to see for our ideal selves, regardless of whether that reflection carries an image in keeping with who we really are. The decisions we make are often motivated by our own interpretation of external influences. We spend a large chunk of time doing things to please everyone else but us. We do everything in our power, often at the expense of our own energy, health and well-being, to live up to the standards that we believe those around us are attaining. We try to prop ourselves up to these impossible standards, simply because that's what we assume will bring us happiness. At the risk of sounding reductive, trying to live up to impossible standards in order to find happiness is a waste of time and energy, motivated by the stories that we tell ourselves regarding life and our role in it. We are the consummate storytellers, often at the expense of our own vision and happiness. The perfect example of what I'm getting at can be found within my own family: my older brother has said that he became a lawyer because he believed that my parents expected it of him, but if you ask my parents if they ever communicated that to him, they will tell you otherwise.

A series of opportunities that gravitate towards us. Many people believe that if we follow the proper channels, opportunities will arise along the way, and our successes will depend on whether or not we take advantage of them. My first career in retail management blossomed out of having taken a sales job in a boutique after dropping out of school in my early twenties. It was there that a head-hunter from a huge international retailer found me and offered me a job, and it was with that retailer that I ended up getting promoted repeatedly throughout the following twelve years. When these opportunities started presenting themselves to me with little or no manipulation on my part, I decided to believe that that was what life was. I was young, not only trying to find my path in life, but also figuring out what the rules of the game were so I could make my way forward. I assumed that the rules were that opportunities would just appear, and that assumption conditioned me to simply accept whatever situation I found myself in, regardless of whether or not I was happy. I figured that something would eventually come along to guide me further towards where I was supposed to be. It was only when I had moved my way to the top of the hierarchy, where the opportunities for advancement that existed no longer interested me, that I began to ask the real questions regarding my own happiness... questions that would challenge me and force me to face my fears, but which eventually led me to a place of clarity and understanding.

By attempting to meet unrealistic standards or by indiscriminately following opportunities, countless numbers of people find themselves chasing happiness, without ever being able to get a firm grasp on it. They wake up after years of "playing the game" to find that they have little to show of any worth to account for the lives they've lived thus far. As a result of this realization, they find themselves re-assessing everything and desperately seeking out guidance and tools to help them evolve and move forward.

Everyone has at least one aspect of their life that they would like to improve. From the relationships with your partner, siblings, workmates, parents and friends to how fulfilling your career is, from the state of your health to your material living conditions, there is something in your life, at least one thing, which you could quickly identify as wanting to be improved upon. And like most other people, you aren't as proactive as you'd like to be in the execution of the changes you'd like to see. People avoid doing something to better their lives for fear of not being good enough or capable enough to see those changes through and have them actually take form, or for fear of losing things already gained. They fear starting the process, only to see it not work out the way they envisioned, bringing them to a place fraught with feelings of failure and inferiority. They prefer waiting to see what unfolds, or they end up going through the motions to bring about change because other people are watching them and they feel the weight of their expectations. Neither of these options is very productive. In fact, they both give the same result: taking a back seat to what you really want for your own life, your own personal evolution.

Instead of basing your decisions on what you expect will make other people like you, the first step in evolving and changing the way you live, is to prioritize your own happiness. This is a call to **change the way you think.** Blatantly. Unapologetically. Regardless of whatever criticism you are afraid to endure, regardless of what you fear other people might think. This is a rebellion. A rebellion against everything that doesn't serve you, that doesn't work for you, that you know needs to change. It is the pursuit of authenticity, purpose, integrity, belonging, and truth. It is you standing up for yourself and what you want for your life. It is about exercising your freedom to be who you are without having to dumb yourself down or make yourself smaller to simply go along with what everyone else seems to be doing. The interesting thing about what is commonly accepted as being good is that it's only good because it's commonly accepted. It doesn't mean it will resonate with you, and it doesn't mean that you're destined to be an outcast just because you find yourself in opposition to the masses. The masses have been wrong on countless occasions, so believe in your own intuition and forget what's commonly believed to be true. It's all relative and subjective.

You need to act in your own best interests and be your own most ardent supporter. This is the skin that you are in. No one else inhabits your shell and the only person you need to answer to is yourself. With that in mind, you need to understand that the only opportunities you should be taking are the ones that bring you closer to your ideal self, the ones that give you a platform from which you can live the life you've dreamed of. These are the ones worth pursuing. Remember that you not only have the power to choose the avenues you'd like to follow; you also have the power to not follow every path that presents itself. You have the power to say no to people, opportunities and avenues that don't resonate with you. This is about honouring who you are and who you want to be, with skill and intention. Following blind leads leaves everything up to chance, and your time is short. Do your best, on purpose, to make sure that what you do is dripping with intention, **dedicating yourself to yourself**, making the most of your time.

THE FIVE ESSENTIAL NEEDS

Are you fulfilled? Do you feel that your needs are being met? Are you even aware of what it is you need that is lacking? Is there something standing in the way of your happiness?

When we feel dissatisfied with the state of our life and start dissecting how we strayed from the path that we thought we'd be on, it can very quickly get overwhelming. Whether it be revisiting past relationships or attempting to recognize and make peace with the patterns that guided us off course, we start obsessing over minute details and can often get caught up in the spiral of criticism and self-judgement.

At the root of all human existence lie five needs that, when met, fulfil us on every level and supply us with the tools we need to move forward with confidence and vision. These five needs are:

1. Sustenance
2. Shelter
3. To love & be loved
4. Connection
5. Stimulation

The first two needs are somewhat self-explanatory, as they are essential to our basic survival. In relation to the third, it's not news to any of us that without love, complicity, partners or like-minded souls to share life with, we'd be helplessly lost. Now, whereas the first three needs are more obvious and straightforward, people are less aware of and familiar with the necessity for the latter two, connection and stimulation.

The fourth need, the need for connection, can be established on two levels: connecting to people and connecting to greater sources of energy.

Connection to people can happen through a life partner with whom you share your most intimate details, or with a group of like-minded people with who you are comfortable enough to exchange on a personal level. When you establish connection in either form, you become aware of your environment and the people around you, which in turn helps you get out of your own daily dramas and the stories that you tell yourself. It helps you get out of your own head. You begin to understand that we are all connected in ways that only become visible through tapping into the collective energy that is found when you are part of a greater number of people, when you are not alone, when you are not dealing only with your own individual personality and energy.

A particular form of connection is rooted in the attention that we pay to each other. There are some beliefs and philosophies that state that the essence of a person changes when attention is paid to them. The most obvious and extreme example of this can be seen with celebrities: once a person attains a certain level of fame, the energy they exude changes, often unbeknownst to them. People I know who have been in the presence of world-famous celebrities have told me that you can't help but look at them, that heads turn towards these public figures often without even having knowledge that they had entered the room. Through the power of our collective attention, we are capable of changing the vibration that another person gives off. Celebrities are fed the power of our attention, which changes their own vibrational energy, and instills in them a sense of belonging, of connection. Having said that, one need not be a celebrity to display vibrational changes from being the object of attention, and that attention need not be on a gobal scale. We've all had one teacher, one friend, one mentor or guru who has given us his or her undivided attention at one point or another, and the majority of us have been forever altered by it for the better.

The other form of connection, this one to a higher energy, can be established in many ways: by identifying and invoking the essence of whatever religion you put your faith in, by going out into nature and connecting to the intensity of the vibration that is found there, or by practicing yoga or meditation or whatever mind/body practice you have. Each of these possibilities provides the space and the opportunity to reflect on the aspects of human existence that we typically don't spend time examining. Regardless of how you do it, connection to what is greater than you is essential because it removes any sense of individuality and aloneness that you may be feeling. It gets you out of the "I" and the "me" and guides you to the "us" and the "we." When you feel connected, any sense of separation disappears and, as we will see further in this book, separation is one of the main root causes of suffering.

In relation to #5 on the list, every single one of us needs to feel stimulated by life, productive, a part of something. Stimulation helps us feel useful and appreciated, reminding us that we have something of worth to offer and that we can make a difference in our immediate environment and the world around us. Stimulation breeds satisfaction and self-esteem, and when this happens, we find the motivation to do and be better than we have in the past.

Feeling stimulated often goes hand in hand with having something to look forward to. At the beginning of every year I lecture to classes about the importance of looking at the 12 months ahead and blocking time out of schedules for vacation or "me-time". I instruct them to literally take a calendar and identify when they would most benefit from a break from their daily responsibilities, then block the time off and do whatever they have to do to make it happen. It can be risky for many people – it means being away from family, from work, from familiarity and routine. It can also pose a financial risk if absence from work means not getting paid, or if money needs to be spent to realize whatever vacation plans were set. I know how important it is to feel like I'm contributing to my workplace and my family, but I also know how burned out I get in both those spheres of my life when I don't plan time and events for myself, away from the rest of it all. Cementing dates and plans always gives me something to look forward to, real hope for whatever adventure lies in wait, and I have found that the more I reflect on these plans, the more stimulated I find myself in my work and relationships.

When the basic needs for love, connection or stimulation do not get met, we start to wander in search of whatever we feel is missing. That sense of disconnection immediately takes precedence over all other aspects of our lives and we find ourselves going to extremes to resolve it. If our efforts prove to be futile, we begin to seek out a sense of satisfaction and reinforcement from other sources, many of them potentially destructive, all to simply feel a sense of worth. We look to food as a source of love. We look to money, to alcohol, to drugs. When one of those needs is not being met and we haven't yet pinpointed what the missing ingredient is, we turn to the substitutes that we know will give us instant and temporary pleasure and gratification, often at the expense of our long-term happiness and well-being.

Eating in copious amounts or eating the things that we know aren't good for us but give us feelings of pleasure are a possible symptom of one of the needs being ignored or unaddressed. When we are depressed, stressed or anxious, we experience chemical changes in the brain that affect one's mood and overall emotional state. Those who are emotional eaters will tend to binge on foods that are not good for them. Eating foods that are high in sugar increases the production of serotonin, which lifts our mood and makes us feel good, which is a good thing, right? Wrong. The high definitely makes us feel better, but it's a temporary fix, gradually waning until it disappears completely, leaving us even more down and out than we were before the serotonin rush. Nonetheless, food is one source of instant gratification that we turn to and have the potential to abuse when one or more of the Five Essential Needs is not being met.

Spending money mindlessly is another way to divert our attention from dealing with what brings us suffering. Think about a time when you went out shopping, buying things you wanted in the moment and getting a thrill. The shopping may have provided you with the high of finding something new to own, but you also know how it felt once you arrived home and took a long look at what you wasted your money on. When we spend money as a way to make us feel better, we end up resenting what we spent the money on and regretting being so irresponsible with our cash. Much like the low that we feel after binge eating, we end up feeling more depressed and anxious after blowing our money on random purchases that can't fill the void created by a need not being met. Blind consumption is just another way of applying a temporary patch to our wounds instead of healing them properly and being able to move on from them.

Abusing alcohol, drugs and engaging in irresponsible sexual activity are other ways in which unhappy people deal with their issues and emotions. The mood altering effects of all these quick fixes help distract us from our problems, but as emotional eating and spending only provide a temporary fix, so do these. Distraction from the source of our unhappiness doesn't solve the problem, it just allows us to take the focus off for a while. Regardless of how long we remain fixated on the distraction, it eventually ends and we find ourselves back at square one, having to face the real sources of our unhappiness. It is through this reliance on the temporary distraction that we create unhealthy affiliations with external variants, affiliations that, if left unchecked, create ongoing dependencies that end up depriving us of happiness and quality of life. We find ourselves living in a hopeless space of routine and mediocrity, convinced that the mundane is all that we deserve when, in fact, we are simply looking to have one or more of the Essential Needs met.

For many, seeking to meet all these needs will seem blatantly self-indulgent. There are always the usual suspects that arise when we attempt to do things for ourselves and our well-being. We may feel a false sense of selfishness and guilt, which partners with the assumption that we won't find the means to make these plans happen. Understand this: if you don't think you will get the time off work, then you won't. If you don't think that you'll find the money to pay for whatever your dreams are, you won't. If you don't think that you will find a life partner, then you won't. Do you understand what I'm getting at? It starts with you. **What you believe will become.** Change the story you've been telling yourself all this time and see just how powerful it can be to actually prove yourself wrong. If you don't invest in what makes yourself truly happy, you will come to a place where you have nothing left to offer those around you. More importantly, however, is the fact that if you don't take any and every opportunity to do something for yourself that will nourish your soul and contribute to your happiness, than you will eventually find yourself completely depleted.

I have often said while teaching a yoga class that if a student is taking a posture but hasn't engaged every limb as an active contributor to the pose, then the pose cannot happen. Every part of the body needs to engage and activate to be able to take and sustain the position. This applies to the five needs in much the same way. If we look at the life we are living as being the sum of many parts, than we can see that if one part is lacking in vitality or isn't being prioritized as much as the others, the greater whole suffers.

It is our responsibility to continuously monitor our behaviours and examine what is happening in our lives, to question not only why it's happening, but whether or not we're responsible for it.

How we may have let it initially grow from a moment to a vice. We must refer back to these five needs in order to identify the ones that are not being met, then do whatever is necessary to reconnect to them. Only then will we have a direction in which we can channel our efforts to find love, joy, contentment and happiness in all facets of our lives.

THE CAUSES OF SUFFERING

Do you feel disconnected from others? Do you feel your friends and family would think less of you if you opened up to them about things that you typically keep to yourself? Do you keep secrets from them for fear of losing their approval? Do you suffer from having to live up to the perception that you or others have about yourself?

I called this project *The Examined Life* for obvious reasons, but I easily could have called it *The Imagined Life*. We are all guilty of telling stories about each other, about the relationships we have with other people, about the world around us, but we're most guilty of telling ourselves **stories about ourselves**. We imagine everything through our perception, and that perception serves to define the world as what we think it is. Your world is the sum total of what you have imagined and defined it to be based on everything you have learned throughout your life's experiences. It is not the same world that any other person sees it as being - every single person has his or her own way of imagining life, and that creation will be different from yours. It is based on the imaginings, the stories we have woven for the world and people around us and our relationship to it and them, but it really is based in the stories we have created about our own individual existences. We tell stories about ourselves to ourselves and then attempt to live up to the roles we've created through those stories.

For example, some people end up being the person everyone comes to for moral support, which allows them to create the story that they are the sympathetic ear for the people around them. Others may find themselves financially supporting family or friends, creating the story for them to believe that they are the financially responsible ones. A popular perception is seeing everyone around us as more capable and successful, achieving the seemingly impossible, which allows us to immediately create and adopt the belief that we are less capable, and thereby inferior. Many of us have inherent tendencies: to offer support, to be compassionate, to be selfish, to feel less intelligent. Once we see these tendencies repeat themselves enough times, we affix labels and adjectives to ourselves, identifying as those things, from which point we no longer carry out the roles naturally. Instead, we identify with the labels and start playing the roles related to them.

> Throughout my childhood, my parents would see a couples' therapist on a regular basis to discuss how things were going with each other and our family. When I was about nine or ten years old they mentioned to me that the therapist had told them that I was the barometer of the family, and that if turmoil was starting to bubble up within our family unit, it would manifest through my words and behaviour.

> Having been told this, I then found myself becoming that barometer by commenting on or reacting to what previously might have simply gone unnoticed. I became what I had been labelled as because I believed and then retold that story to myself. Of course that wasn't the sum total of who I considered myself to be, but in those barometric moments, I voluntarily wore that label which put undue pressure on me to live up to that role.

No one is ever one thing and there are countless facets to the same being. When we carry around labels (*i.e.* depressed, supportive, lying, inferior, sad, hopeful, afraid) we end up cheating ourselves into letting many positive aspects of our personalities fall by the wayside. We also give ourselves the permission to stay stuck in the past. Think about it: if you have identified yourself as an inherently shy person, then you start to believe the myth that you have created for yourself. You therefore go through your life playing up the shyness, so that it no longer comes from a place of genuine authenticity, but rather from a place of feeling the need to live up to the persona you've created for yourself. Doing this attaches you to that persona, which in turn keeps you from evolving and allowing your personality to grow. We are never simply one thing, so if we attach to one thing and hide behind it, we are stunting our own natural growth and evolution. Allowing this to happen is like taking a promotion in a career that no longer makes you happy: you take the promotion because it's safe and easy to stay in the environment you're familiar with, and it possibly comes with perks, such as a rise in salary and stature. When you allow this to happen, it keeps you from whatever possibilities lie ahead because you don't have the time, energy or attention span to execute your new duties while keeping an eye open for newness. You have to make room for whatever you hope life will bring you, and so if you label yourself as one thing and then attach to it, you are voluntarily preventing yourself from growing into the person you would like to become.

Many of the labels that we affix to ourselves stem from our insecurities. Some of us go through life keeping secrets about habits, self-image, flaws, sexuality, desires or addictions. We become paralysed by the fear that if the secret became common knowledge, we would suffer terrible embarrassment and shame. Some of us walk around carrying the shame of past events and the reactions they provoked. We get through difficult moments by doing whatever we need to, and then feel terrible shame regarding our actions when looking back on them. What we end up doing, in reality, is becoming our own executioner, because by continuing to live with the weight of our own judgement and opinions, we treat ourselves worse than we'd be treated by others if they knew what we were dealing with. Those of us who have been or are currently motivated by our insecurities need to understand a few things. Firstly, in many cases, our reactions to events, especially stressful or traumatic ones, are completely instinctual - our brains are hard-wired to react in certain ways regardless of whether we think the reaction is an appropriate or honourable one, and so what we need to understand is that it's not personal. We will react how we need to react in order to survive, and to judge how that happens is to believe that we have more control than the brain does. It's a losing battle, every single time. Secondly, if we made more of an effort to share our lives with the people around us, if we paid more attention to what everyone else is dealing with in their lives, we'd realize that they also have their own issues with insecurities, vices, flaws, guilt, self-loathing, shame.

What most of us need to hear is that every single person suffers from something. That the human condition is based in suffering. The cause may be different from one person to another, but the symptoms are the same for all of us. Don't get me wrong, human nature (the state we are all born into) is joy, but the human condition is to suffer. Amongst other faiths, religions and belief systems, Hinduism and Buddhism define human suffering as the consequence of us not being aware that the nature of life as we know it is **transformation**. We suffer because we resist change. We suffer because we fight what is. Change is the only constant we can count on, so when we fight change, we fight what is. This results in suffering, each and every time. Suffering also occurs when we believe that we are separate from our siblings, from our parents, from the world around us. We walk around telling ourselves that no one could ever understand our suffering, leaving us alone and isolated. We compare ourselves to others, holding them up and keeping ourselves down. **We create our own hell** by choosing to accept that we are uglier, less capable, dumber and less interesting than everyone else. We choose to accept this, and when we do, we immediately fall victim to the timeless (and unsubstantiated) belief **that we are on our own**.

All suffering can be traced back to one moment in time where something occurred resulting in feeling separate from the rest, apart and alone. Those struggling with anxiety or depression feel totally isolated, as do those with eating disorders, body dismorphia, chemical dependencies, addictions of all sorts, and general anxieties and insecurities. The second we feel separate from the greater whole, we feel like there is something missing, like we're incomplete. That sense of being incomplete comes from feeling separate from the energy that unites everyone. There is an energy that pervades every single thing in existence. Without ever being taught to be, we are a part of this connection from the day we are conceived. We remain not only connected to this energy for our entire life, but we literally embody it as well, because we exist. The simple fact that we exist serves as a tie that binds us to all else that exists. That seed of energy is within us and all around us, contained in everything that is. Understanding this instantly changes how we see the world around us and our place in it, because we find ourselves, all of a sudden, part of a much bigger collective entity. It is, however, commonly understood through various faiths and belief systems that this unity that has existed before any of us is masked by the illusion of separation.

When we feel ashamed, we feel separate. When we feel sad, it's because we feel separate. The same goes for when we feel guilty, embarrassed, too fat, too thin, too tall, too short, too dumb, too smart, too ugly, etc. When we feel too *anything*, a separation occurs from that energy that typically keeps us navigating our way through life with ease and discriminative wisdom. In order to combat the effects of this sense of being apart, one must first be able to maintain a presence of mind alert enough to recognize when any given stimulus prompts that disconnect. Whenever an emotion of inferiority, or even superiority for that matter, gets triggered, one must be able to recognize what's happening in that moment. Total presence is required. With that focus, one can purposefully redirect attention onto whatever signs of unity are around, instead of going the easy route of buying into the feelings of separateness and then following them down the path that leads only to loneliness and feeling less-than. By choosing to see unity where separation tries to place itself, we succeed in choosing happiness and connection over misery and separateness.

What no one tells us, and what I'm here to get across to you, is that everyone suffers and feels separate at some point. There are obviously variants under the umbrella term of suffering, *i.e.* money issues, eating disorders, psychological disorders, gender and sexuality issues, I could go on and on. The heart of the matter is that we obsess over life, death, and everything that happens in between the two in the form of our daily dramas. No one is spared this cycle of suffering and destructive behaviour. It's when we finally wake up to the realization that we're exhausted from the non-stop kineticism of our mental activity that we begin to yearn for guidance to help us stop the cycle. It's when we choose to focus on what we share as oppposed to what separates us that we will find true, lasting peace and happiness.

We can continue to contribute to our suffering by identifying others as different and separate, or we can look deeper than the obvious and realize that through the concept of existing, there is actually no separation at all. We co-exist with everything and everyone, and it's through that co-existence that we understand that what affects one of us affects every one of us. We can choose to understand that everything and everyone around us has something in common: we are here. We exist. We may look different, the frequency of the vibrations that hold our forms together may differ, and the vibrations in us and around us may not be the same, but don't fool yourself, we all exist. Every thing and every one. Like the invisible chemical bonds that keep everything in the world in a co-dependent state of being, so we are co-dependent. That alone gives us something that binds us together, a thread of continuity that reminds us that we are a part of something bigger than each one of us. We have the choice as to whether we want to focus on our differences or on the things that we share. We have the choice to make our way through life as a collective whole or as a collection of individuals. Despite having all the tools and technology to bring us together, we still seem have difficulty connecting.

The bottom line is this: you can stop the cycle of suffering by not allowing your stories to continue to overshadow the positive aspects of your life; you can acknowledge that everyone suffers from something instead of letting your secrets keep you isolated; you can seek out what you have in common with others and the world around you instead of focusing on the alienating differences. Ultimately, the most important tool you need to be able to reach for in moments of suffering is the knowledge that everything is in a state of flux. Everything is constantly changing, transforming, often without us even being aware of it. Who we are in one moment will change, how we feel in one moment will change, and how we see the world around us will change. The only thing we can truly bank on is that **change will continue to occur.** Stop fighting it. Sit back and enjoy the ride. Remain open to seeing what lies just around the bend and stop labelling yourself. All the tools to end or at least alleviate your suffering are available to you once you've learned to recognize and handle them.

THE SELFISHNESS OF THE EGO

What is the ego? Have you ever been told to detach from your ego? Do you find your feelings are easily hurt by others? Do you easily get disappointed when others act in ways you don't expect?

The most hashed-around advice that is constantly given is to detach from the ego. To let go of it. To stop allowing it from encouraging us to make ourselves feel better by seeking out temporary and material fixes. To stop comparing ourselves to everyone and everything else around us. The nucleus of that advice is brilliant, actually. We should all let go of the hold that the ego has on us. We should be focusing on what binds us together instead of what separates us. That is the ultimate ambition. By doing so, we focus on our collective experience and forget our differences. But if you really think about it, asking someone to detach from their ego is like asking someone who has never gone jogging before to throw on a pair of trainers and run a marathon. The exceptional among us will be able to do it, but the rest of us who need measurable goals will fall short and get discouraged in the process. So for all of you doing that incredibly relevant ego-work, here's what I have to offer: instead of telling yourself that you have to detach from the ego, why not ask yourself to simply detach from the selfishness of the ego?

Yes, the craving of the **ego is responsible for suffering**. When we pursue that which the ego deems pleasing and it eludes us, we suffer. When we don't get the ego stroke we so rabidly seek out, we suffer. When we are used to getting the ego stroke and it all of a sudden ceases to rise up to meet us, we suffer. Our egos constantly want to be fed by hearing how fantastic, charming, talented, intelligent, good-looking, funny, capable and charismatic we are. It can never get enough, and if we somehow come to a place where we believe that to feed the selfishness of the ego is to become more of all the compliments it craves, then we fall into a dangerous trap of superficialities and miss the point entirely.

The ego, however, can also be a source of love, confidence, vision, determination and light. Appreciation of beauty is ego-based, as is falling into a love powerful enough to sustain people for their entire lives. Think about it - the word "love" can represent what we extend **outwards**, selflessly and organically, or it can evoke feelings of possessiveness as we search for someone to love, and once found, to defend as our own. In many cases, the ego is what gets us through the door, but once that happens, we need tools to keep us in the room. The selfishness of the ego will not keep us in the room for very long, so why not re-focus our efforts on decontaminating the ego by removing the selfish desires that motivate our behaviors? Seek out newness, incorporate humility, and feel gratitude towards what we are already blessed with in our lives. The ego, by definition, is **limitation**. It limits by convincing us that things are what it wants them to be for its own selfish purposes, instead of allowing us to see the reality of what is in front of us. It prevents us from seeing the ties that unite us, opting instead to trick us into believing that the separation we sense is the ultimate reality.

Another way that the ego limits us is by tricking us into believing that our friends and romantic partners are who the ego has defined them as being. The process is simple: we meet someone, and immediately suss them out, label them, discriminate, categorize and compare, all based on the information we've already got stored in our frame of reference. Once the ego is satisfied with its assessment, we have a clear, defined idea of who the other person is. Whether or not we're aware of it, the rest of our relationship with that person is spent trying to make them live up to the ego's initial assessment, despite the glaring fact that they were never exactly that person to begin with. This becomes most obvious once a friend or partner does something that we simply cannot wrap our brain around. We feel personally affected by the action, and wonder how well we could have known someone if that person was capable of doing something that seemed so "out of character." It wasn't actually "out of character," it was simply not part of the biased persona that we had created for them.

Truthfully speaking, we make people out to be who we need them to be so that we can be comfortable with them. We do the same thing with everything that we come into contact with. Anything that seems diametrically opposed to what pleases us or that threatens or challenges the ego becomes something to avoid. We attach to what proves to be pleasurable and we avoid what doesn't. We avoid people who challenge us or who make us feel badly about ourselves. Again, this brings us back to the selfishness of the ego. If someone we meet constantly mocks us, then it's only normal to want to distance ourselves from that source of mockery. The ego wants to be fed, not knocked down. However, if we find ourselves wanting to distance ourselves from someone whose physical appearance, talent, or charisma makes us feel inferior, then we have to examine how we are allowing the selfishness of the ego to trigger jealousy, envy and other emotions that make us feel "less than". Identifying in someone else something that we want, and allowing that identification to drum up feelings of **criticism** and **judgement** of ourselves and others, is essentially validating the ego's impression. And at the risk of being repetitive, attaching to the idea of who someone is, or what a situation might be, will always pull you away from what actually is, as the selfishness of the ego tricks you into believing what helps it stay inflated.

> Working in the yoga community has proven to be something of an eye-opener. My intentions going into this industry were manifold. I wanted to help people heal, physically and otherwise. I also wanted to create opportunities for myself to travel to incredible destinations while bringing people along who might never have taken the time or the money to take the trips on their own. Holding yoga retreats met these two objectives. I dove into my new career with abandon, passionate and ambitious for the first time ever in my professional life. I soon saw that the community I found myself in was polarized by the constant scrutiny yoga teachers are under from other yoga teachers. Who's doing what, how successful are they, how do I compare to what they're doing? I felt a real disconnect, so I got involved with a community organisation

> that was planning a yoga event. The efforts and results were satisfying, but didn't change anything. In fact things went in the wrong direction. Finding myself immersed in that energy, I started catching myself doing the same thing! I started gauging how I was doing based on what other teachers were doing, and allowing moments of inferiority or resentment to creep in. I've sinced stopped that pattern, choosing only to focus on my own intentions and projects, knowing I'm fulfilling my goals and dreams, living my dharma, and not trying to measure up. I still find that instead of coming together as a community of people who do the same thing and can share individual experiences and anecdotes, the accepted way is to stay separate and remain focused on individual interests. It is the craving and selfishness of each individual's ego that allows them to judge and criticize what makes them feel inferior, and subsequently causes division.

When we allow the selfishness of the ego to dictate how we treat and judge others, we unconsciously permit them to behave the same way back to us. If we treat others badly because our ego feels the need to exert power or superiority, then we are unconsciously agreeing that it's ok to be judged and criticised until everyone is existing independently of each other. The selfishness of the ego divides through its limitation, and it's time we woke up to that fact and took charge of our own lives with enough clarity to understand that we are stronger and better off united, working and evolving as a collective entity. We are stronger together, managing every aspect of our lives without claiming ownership or proprietary rights over any of it.

WHO YOU ARE

How do you define who you are? Do the responsibilities you carry out and the job titles you hold in your career factor into who you believe yourself to be? What about your responsibilities to your family and friends? When all your responsibilities have been carried out and there are no distractions, who are you?

As technology allows us to stay in contact with one another with ever-increasing frequency, we find ourselves oscillating between longer working hours and trying to get everything taken care of in all other aspects of our lives. Our task lists keep getting longer and longer, with unanswered emails and text messages piling up, all of which take up more and more time until we find ourselves collapsing at the end of the day. As moments when we can simply be still and breathe become harder and harder to come by, we gradually lose sight of who we really are, and the lunacy of it all is that we, as a society of evolved beings, have decided that to do so is acceptable. There is an increased pace to daily life which threateningly demands that we keep up, or lose out. So we do our best to keep up, at the expense of our well-being. The struggle to keep that frenetic lifestyle is exactly that - a struggle. It exhausts us and demands too much of our attention and effort, and without sheer force of will, combined with the not-unrelated rise in consumption of coffee and energy drinks, we'd simply run out of fuel. This process is the epitome of suffering, of a living hell - we're running around just trying to keep up with the current, and in the process we are forgetting ourselves, losing sight of **who we are**.

The truth of who you have been up to this point in your life lies in the space that exists between what you believe and how you behave. The gap between the two is slimmer for some, and incredibly vast for others, and in many cases, that truth is not something you'd necessarily advertise or reveal to the people in your life. However, it is imperative to identify what that truth of your past behaviour is and accept it as being a big part of your personality and reality in order to move forward with your personal evolution and grow into the person you are meant to be. You cannot move onto the next stage of your life with authenticity without acknowledging and accepting your past. You need to know where you've been before you can assess where you are going, and as is the case for many people, what you find yourself doing when no one is watching plays a huge role in getting to know and accept yourself.

The older you get, the less time you feel you have to accomplish the things that you'd like to do in your lifetime. Our teens and twenties are all about trying to find our way: to establish a career, to meet and connect with people, to find a partner, to prove our worth to friends and family by assimilating smoothly and seamlessly into society... basically, to transition from adolescence into what's commonly accepted as adulthood. Those years are spent trying to fit into everyone else's standards and rising to the challenge. If this has been your experience and you lived it without feeling the freedom or confidence required to incorporate your personality into the process, then it's fair to assume that you eventually grew tired of the facade. This effort to perform generally continues uninterrupted until something gives out; it could be a professional burnout, a breakdown, or a general loss of patience for everything and everyone around you. Regardless of how it manifests, these scenarios are all missing one key ingredient: your authentic personality. Who you believe yourself to be. Not when you're trying to impress your boss, or when you're trying to fill your bank account, not when you're starving yourself to look a certain way, or when you're pretending to be someone else to win the approval of others. Only when you allow your essence, your personality, all the elements that make up who you are, to be included into what you spend the majority of your time doing, will you find the endurance and balance necessary to perform your duties on a long-term basis. But are you really aware of who you are?

Your identity can only be superficially defined by the scenarios mentioned above. The fact that you do the things you do in pursuit of whatever your goals are tells you certain things, gives you tidbits of information about what you're willing to do to get what you want. It doesn't, however, completely define you. Who you really are is largely based on the feelings, thoughts, sensations and beliefs you experience when you're alone and no one is watching. When you're having a party for one, who is that person?

There seems to be a growing reaction to the hypocrisy of the standards our society continues to uphold. Politicians are judged by their personal life instead of their ability to successfully guide and manage the constituencies they are responsible for, and if they slip just a little bit, if they show the slightest bit of humanity, they are torn down and destroyed by the onslaught of judgment and disdain thrown their way. The same is true of anyone who falls into the celebrity machine that comes with being a public figure. Singers, teachers, actors, authors, religious leaders, athletes and business people have all felt the thrill of the high from becoming hugely successful and visible, and have eventually, at one point or another, suffered the downward spiral of being torn down by the same people who built up their celebrity. Essentially, we hold celebrities up to a superhuman standard, and when they prove themselves incapable of living up to it, we destroy them. We live by the "do as I say, not as I do" adage, expecting others to be capable of embodying all the attributes we'd like to see in ourselves, but aren't capable of upholding in our own lives. Instead of understanding that we can't live up to the standard because it's not a realistic one, we create the story that we're not disciplined or capable enough, and look to celebrities and public figures to be stronger than us. We strip them of the humanity that we permit ourselves to have, and when they prove to be every bit as human as we are, the tsunami of disappointment erupts from us as a wave of judgment and disgust, and we stand by the sidelines as their star falls back down to earth. Sounds insane, no? Well there's something even more insane than that. **We are also guilty of doing the same thing to ourselves.**

When we run ourselves ragged trying to be the model employee, family member, and friend, we're bound to eventually run out of steam. In the process of being everything to everyone, we end up being nobody to ourself. Our effort gets directed into making everyone else happy while ignoring what we want and need. As far as approaches to life go, it's a weak one, one that has a limited shelf life. It can't go on forever, because it's not our natural state. Our natural state is to be connected to our soul, to our essence, to who we are. When we try to suppress that natural state of being by donning the hats and personas necessary to live up to everyone else's standards, we strip ourselves of our identity. We lose sight of who we are. And that depletes us of that spark that makes us happy, that keeps us in a perpetual state of hope in the world and our place in it. It strips us of joy, which is our natural state and creates the feeling of being separate. When we finally break down and come to a screeching halt due to the absence of joy in our life, we feel disappointed by and in ourselves. We become the celebrities we admired from afar and ended up destroying. We come down as hard on ourselves as we have done with others, often harder, actually, and we judge and criticize our inability to maintain a standard that was unattainable to begin with. We treat ourselves as we would our own worst enemy - with hypocrisy, judgment, and disdain, all because we didn't allow our true nature, our true personality to be included into our daily life. It all stems from not being accustomed to pay attention to who we are in moments of privacy and stillness, and to then honour who we find ourselves being by making room for that person in our careers and relationships. It is in those moments when we can identify and accept who we are, who we can't help but being. And when armed with that knowledge, we can then proceed with truth, clarity, and honesty.

Not being afraid to assume our personality changes everything. It draws people to us for all the right reasons. Being transparent and authentic will not only have the people around us love us for who we are, but it serves as an example to follow. Most people pretend to be who they are not in order to make everyone else happy.

When they see someone confident in their own skin, it motivates them to find their own truth, because it's that confidence that informs everything. Relationships change, job satisfaction and performance change. Overall happiness increases from redirecting the energy previously spent on maintaining facades into a life of authenticity.

Actions speak louder than words. You can tell yourself and the people you communicate with whatever you think makes you look good or whatever you think you or they want to hear, but the truth of who you are is in many ways determined by what you experience, how you behave, and what you do with your time when there's no one looking. That truth can often be something you'd never want anyone to see or know about because you know that it may not portray you in the most flattering of lights, but it doesn't make it any less true. If that is what exists, then let it simply be.

THE WAYS WE CLING

What relationships, stories or assumptions are you holding onto at the expense of your own personal evolution? Conversely, what are you avoiding because you know it will make you uncomfortable or leave you feeling challenged?

If you take a step back from your life and objectively observe what you've experienced up to this moment, you'll begin to see various patterns emerge in your behaviour. When seen with a certain amount of distance and perspective, what emerges from these patterns is how you consciously or unconsciously gravitate to whatever sources of pleasure you find yourself exposed to, and how you keep a distance from the people, places and situations that leave you with feelings of discomfort or challenge.

Every single one of us gravitates towards the things, places, and people that make us feel good. Whether it be a promotion at work that would potentially give us the adulation and congratulations of our peers, or the attention of someone we find attractive or impressive, we hone in on that which brings us pleasure and makes us feel good. Once we get a taste of that pleasurable sensation, the selfishnes of the ego quickly forms an attachment to its source, and that attachment then grows into a craving to relive and repeat the experience, thereby glorifying the source as that which brings us happiness. Throughout life, we are repeatedly encouraged to seek out pleasure from external sources, but what we are not encouraged to do, however, is identify that attachment and craving as a potential obstacle on our journey towards real happiness.

Picture it: if you do a task in your job really effectively and you get showered with praise and positive reinforcement, then even on an unconscious level, the next time you execute a task, you have the memory of the praise/reward/positive reinforcement in the back of your mind as a motivator for the work you're currently doing. This not only changes the essence and intention of the work, but it sets you up for disappointment when you don't get the ego stroke you were expecting. Even if the work is of equal or superior quality to its predecessor, it's extremely possible that you won't get as much fanfare or congratulations for it, and when the outcome doesn't meet the expectation, you suffer disappointment, wondering what you did wrong, causing insecurity to mount. The ego takes a bit of a blow and you immediately fall into the trap of thinking that you will get what you need by seeking your happiness from external sources. You crave to repeat the event. Having mistaken the pleasurable sensation as true happiness, you expend time, energy and resources looking to relive it. You chase it, and end up clinging to it, thinking that it will bring you happiness when you can eventually get it back into your grasp. It can take a very long time to realize that this approach doesn't really lead to anything permanently satisfying, and will put distance between you and your center of peace and neutrality.

We do the same thing as we strive to avoid scenarios, people and places that make us feel challenged or uncomfortable. If we know that something we have experienced has brought about feelings of disappointment or inferiority, then it's only normal to want to avoid going through the same events, knowing that they have already brought us suffering in varying degrees. In our attempts to distance ourselves from the source of the discomfort, we are in effect creating a bond to that avoidance and, essentially, glorifying it. We demonize it, manipulating it as something with the potential to destabilize us, and we then make efforts to stay away from it.

Attaching to sources of pleasure or avoiding sources of discomfort keeps us from finding a place of openness and neutrality - we stay honed in on whatever we like or dislike, and we end up defining them in whatever ways suit our purposes. We make things out to be what we think they are, when in actuality, we are fabricating all of it. We create stories out of nothing, and those stories end up influencing what decisions we make in life. We react to what we think exists instead of being open to what actually is. If we could simply remain open to whatever happens, we would start to gain clarity, enough to see that every single thing that happens around and to us is a messenger of sorts, manifesting to teach us something. Being open and ready for whatever happens prevents us from forming habits that keep us running towards or away from what we think will affect us. Letting things happen and welcoming everything simply allows us to break patterns, let go of the identity and stories that we have applied to ourselves, and learn just how capable we actually are in any given situation with enough clarity to react to what actually is, as opposed to reacting to what we think will happen. If we previously thought ourselves better off by avoiding a certain type of situation, but then allow ourselves to simply receive it again if it happens to present itself, we might find ourselves not repeating the mistakes that originally brought us to a bad place. Life will constantly and consistently surprise us, if given the chance to be experienced from a place of openness and receptivity to whatever happens. Every single moment in time that enters our sphere of awareness is there for a reason and is meant to bring information. These moments and events are teachers, there to have us walk away with more information about the world and our life within it than we previously had.

Something that we have all done at some point in each of our lives is to cling to something that brings temporary pleasure, but actually is not good for us on any level. How many of us have dated people who gave us that thrill, that feeling of being alive, with every sense heightened and every cell in our body attracted to the rush of simply being with that person, despite knowing that he or she was not good for us? Celebrities have built careers on embodying the bad-boy/bad-girl essence, knowing that the attraction they work so hard to create eventually pulls in the most straight-laced and reluctant among us. From people to alcohol to chemicals to shopping to food, many people attach to things that aren't good for them, but don't know how to start the process of disentangling themselves from their vice.

There are ancient Hindu scriptures that state that the "the good is one thing, the pleasant another... the wise prefer the good to the pleasant." So how do we differentiate between the good and the pleasant? Typically the pleasant is pleasant for oneself alone. The good benefits more than the individual. So in trying to assess the validity of what we believe is good for us, we can ask if the people who know us also benefit from what we're living. If they don't, if they would be hurt or disappointed or insulted by what we think is good, then perhaps it's only pleasant in the short term, but bad in the long term. It can be extremely dangerous to continuously follow paths in life based on what feels good. This approach takes into consideration only what is good for you, often at the expense of others. We should always be weighing what the effects of our actions and words will be, especially on those around us. If we can become accustomed to making decisions based on the greater good, then we have a responsibility to do it.

Your goal is peace of mind. Regardless of how each of you defines or verbalizes it, you are, within yourself, throughout your day-to-day life, seeking peace. Peace is your natural state, from which you have grown. If you truly want to find it, then you have to understand that to gravitate towards something repeatedly because it brings you what you believe is pleasure is to potentially move further away from what you're seeking. To constantly avoid what you think will make you feel badly also moves you away from serenity. In both instances, there is an intentional expenditure of energy to manipulate events to be how you think they should be. Ask yourself if your situation is good for you alone or for the greater good. If the former applies, trust that what feels good in the moment often brings you away from peacefulness in your life. I'm not talking about the occasional indulgement in a dessert or a shopping spree. I'm talking about the habits and tendencies that, when examined, you know are bringing you away from the peace of mind you seek. If you know that you are innately peaceful, and that the undercurrent of peace is always with you, even when things get a little crazy, then **you always have it to focus on and come back to** when the crazy gets out of hand. With it, you will always land on your feet. You can learn to check yourself the moment you notice that you are gravitating towards something that drags you away from your center, as well as when you find yourself avoiding dealing with something or someone. The quest for peace and serenity is never-ending, one that brings valuable lessons and that requires focus and awareness of one's habits and tendencies. Make peace your priority.

WE'RE HERE, AND IT'S NOW

Are you bored with your life? Do you feel that every day is a carbon copy of the previous one, with minor details changing occasionally? Do you consider yourself to be lucky?

We love escapism. We flock to the movie theatres, immerse ourselves in games, the internet, gossip magazines, television programs and books to simply break from getting bored. Like many other things, escapism isn't a bad thing in moderation. However, if we spend too much time out of the here and now, disconnected from our life, we are standing in the way of our own happiness. We need to get out of our heads and open our eyes. We need to connect more to what's going on around us and be receptive to opportunities, instead of letting every precious minute we've been honoured with pass us by. We need to connect to the present moment, because the effects of doing so are more vital to our happiness than we know.

Here: Connecting to the present moment involves looking for newness. When I was a teenager, I typically walked around with my shoulders hunched and my gaze down on the sidewalk. My grandmother, one of the brightest souls I've ever met, was the one who finally (and literally) shoved her knuckle into my spine, forcing me to look up, look ahead, look around, and be aware of what I was missing. She taught me to stand up straight and look people in the eyes. The lesson was invaluable and has stayed with me ever since. We are all guilty of walking with our heads down. We all have a tendency to go through life with our thoughts stuck elsewhere. **With your eyes open, look around and actively seek out what you've never noticed before.** There's a difference between having your eyes open and using them to actually see. Staying stuck in your thoughts is like lowering a gauzy film over your eyes – everything's still visible, but somewhat obscured. Lift the gauze and see what and who you are surrounded by. The rewards of searching for newness in the familiar are manifold. We become connected to the world and events unfolding around us, and we step into a place of readiness for the opportunities that we are surrounded by in any given moment.

Now: We all walk around lost in thought that is based in the past or the future, but rarely in the present. Meditation teaches that 85-90% of our thoughts are focused on the past or the future, and the majority of them are of no use. They are useless for two reasons: they are not referred back to when trying to avoid repeating negative patterns or decisions, nor are they useful when making plans for the future. They are simply a waste of time. **This is about understanding that the only thing we know about the past is that it's done, and the only thing we know about the future is that it will be different**. A very effective exercise that I've practised is to catch myself while daydreaming and immediately assess whether what I was thinking about was actually useful or not. More often than not, it wasn't. I was wasting my time on a past that I couldn't change or a future that might not even come to pass. None of it was useful, just distracting.

If walking with your head up, eyes alert and open doesn't resonate with you, then try this: **make a list of things you know would be good for you but don't want to do, and then do them.** Dealing with things that scare, intimidate or challenge us helps keep us focused on the present moment, our senses heightened, our attention undivided. Purposefully doing things that we don't normally do not only keeps us in the present moment, it opens pathways in the brain, which in turn keeps us alert and observant.. It also helps us learn the extent to which we are capable of accomplishing what may have seemed impossible in the past and getting the gratifying reward that comes with it. The more we accomplish what we never would have believed possible shows us just how limitless our options are in this lifetime, allowing us to set goals that will see our loftiest ambitions and wildest dreams accomplished, creating the best life we could live, all by bringing ourselves back into the present moment as often as possible.

If we focus on staying in the present moment, with our heads up and eyes open, we will see so much more than we think exists, which, ultimately, is what separates people who consider themselves **lucky** versus those who consider themselves **unlucky**. Now bear with me for a moment as I delve into the concept of luck. For the purpose of this book, I am not using the word "luck" to represent the randomness behind winning the lottery or being the millionth customer at the supermarket. Luck is simply having the presence of mind required to recognize newness and the **possibilities** contained therein. In essence, we make our own luck through the steps and effort that bring us to any given moment and place in time and by having the presence of mind to be aware of it.

Many people who consider themselves unlucky are guilty of not noticing the opportunities surrounding them at any given moment because their attention is stuck in useless thoughts. If our time is spent distracted, we're not living fully, because we remain isolated in the past or the future. What this inevitably leads to is the creation of the story that we tell ourselves. "I'm not a lucky person, nothing good ever happens to me." And as we've seen earlier, the more we label something, the more we see it as that. We become what we believe. If we walk around with our heads down, lost in all things other than the present moment, then we're not seeing the opportunities around us. Conversely, if we walk with our heads up and eyes open, actively seeking out newness in what would otherwise appear to be routine and insignificant, then we are awake to any and all opportunities that come our way. **We must come back to the present moment.**

Another benefit to staying connected to the here and now is that we become more aware of our surroundings and potential sources of danger. I have been in 2 car accidents and 2 scooter accidents and I can honestly confess that each accident occurred because my mind was elsewhere. I was visualizing where I was headed, creating possible scenarios out of the meetings I had scheduled, going over conversations and moments that had already occurred. My eyes were open, but I was too busy trapped in my thoughts to see what was going on around me. Every accident was a wake-up call for me to **come back to the now**. To not only **look** around me, but **see** what was there. Wandering away from the events that happen in real time around us not only deprives us of fully experiencing them, but potentially puts us at risk.

For some, seeking out newness may seem ridiculous, an infantile way to trick ourselves into adopting new behaviours. To those people, I offer this: the second we fall into patterns and routines, the mind wanders and we're gone. To look for newness is to stay in a place of presence and humility - to approach everything, even the most mundane, well-studied or familiar, as a student who knows nothing. One who knows nothing is always open and ready for those oft-fleeting glimpses of opportunity, hope, truth, beauty, and love.

We begin life by experiencing a sequence of firsts... and then we end up steeped in routine. We find ourselves going through the same motions every day, to the point where the monotony becomes our new normal. When did this become acceptable? And how can the familiar and recognizable in the present moment be rediscovered? The more we yank ourselves out of the past and the future and into the present, the more we walk with our heads up, the more newness we will see. And the more we seek out newness in the familiar, the more we become alert to possibilities and opportunities. When we continuously come back to the mindset of a child or a student – someone with curiosity, a connection to whatever is happening in front of them, and a willingness to learn - we finally understand that there is so much more to experience and absorb. We begin to live life as it should be lived: fully, with presence and curiosity, but most of all, with a sense of readiness for whatever comes our way.

THE PAST EXAMINED

Do you suspect that you may be dragging past events that hurt or traumatized you into your present-day life? Are these events preventing you from finding happiness? How much is your past affecting your present and, potentially, your future?

Many of us can pinpoint a moment, usually in the developmental years of childhood or adolescence, when something happened to or around us which massively imprinted itself into our personality and our frame of reference. This moment is when we felt the first semblance of separation take place from our loved ones and our environment. From infancy to young adulthood, the majority of us are highly emotional beings, impacted viscerally when anything out of the ordinary occurs. Regardless of how much time passes between the incident and the present day, many people feel the depth of the original impact, allowing the emotional imprint of the experience to not only stay with them, but to influence the choices they make throughout adulthood.

I was raised by parents who not only loved their children, but passionately loved each other, and still do to this day. Many of my friends, however, were not so fortunate, and I saw them deal with the effects of parents divorcing and families splintering apart. Some of those friends are still in my life today, and throughout our friendships I have seen the residual effects of their issues with trust and abandonment bubble up, altering their ability to accurately and objectively gauge the health of their relationships and the intentions of their partners. In many cases, those issues proved to be the downfall of potentially great unions, simply because the hurt that had been inflicted so many years back when witnessing their parents split up was innocently triggered by their mate. This is just one example of how one's past can affect one's future – divorce, death of a loved one, accidents, illnesses, physical abuse or impediment – they all hold the potential to scar and stay with us throughout the rest of our lives if left unexamined.

If this resonates with you, then understand that the only way to move past whatever you're dealing with is to identify the **facts** relating to the incident and separate the **emotions** you've attached to them. One needs to be able to objectively identify events to be able to process them, as if the events themselves had happened to someone else and were being reported on.

> A friend of mine lost her life in the North Tower of the World Trade Center in New York City on September 11, 2001, and when I found out that she had been killed, I went through months of insomnia, emotional turmoil and shock. The grief at losing her merged with the horror of how she died, which then merged with the trauma of the media's incessant bombard-

ment of images and reporting which prevented me from starting to heal.

Losing Chantal brought me right back to when I first felt true grief for the death of my childhood babysitter who died in a car accident. That loss of innocence, that dawning and sudden realization of the darkness that life could potentially have in store for us, came right back to me. After allowing those sensations to overtake me, I had to eventually force myself to separate what I was feeling from what the facts were relating to the attack on the towers, and Chantal's presence there that day. Don't get me wrong – the process affected me on such a visceral level that the emotional wounds took years to start healing. To this day, I have trouble seeing footage or images of the events, or even listening to songs that I associate with that specific moment in time. I have, however, been able to deal with what happened and the loss of a true friend. It was only when I sat myself down and separated my grief and shock from the cold, hard facts that I felt myself slowly moving past the trauma of it all. Once I was able to get my brain around the insanity of what had actually happened, and trust me, it took a long time to make sense of the horror that airplanes had flown into buildings which I had visited only 3 weeks earlier, and that one of my friends had been in one of the buildings as it happened, I was then able to compassionately handle my reactions to it all. It was in doing so that I could start to move past it all and remember Chantal for who she was and not simply for how she died.

It is with this intention that the most scarring of events can be dealt with and laid to rest. We are not inherently programmed with all the tools we need to make our way through life unscathed, and we don't know everything about ourselves or the world we operate in. What we feel early on in life can make a surprisingly lasting impression on us, an impression that gets revisited as similar scenarios unfold throughout the rest of our life, triggering the initial imprints that were created as we experienced "firsts" in our youth. The first step towards changing reactionary behavior is to identify how and when you were deeply affected by events in your past. Trying to tap into how it felt in the moment is key to recognizing whether that same reaction re-appears in your current friendships or relationships.

Consider this: if as a young child you were pushed down in the playground by another child, you might have a tendency to dislike playgrounds, or even other children. The feelings of hurt, rejection, and inferiority that arose from being bullied manifested as soon as you hit the ground. As you grow older, you take that dislike for playgrounds and children into your adult life, allowing the emotions associated with the event to affect you. If this prevents you from enjoying the company of children or from allowing your own child to play in a park, then what needs to be done is to look at the original incident objectively. Someone pushed you down. You were bullied. That's it. It's that simple. It happens in parks, playgrounds, homes and schoolyards all over the world. What happens when we get pushed down? Ideally, we stand back up and keep going. Maybe we protest being pushed down. Maybe we try to push the aggressor down for revenge. Regardless, what affected you wasn't being pushed down; it was the jolt of emotions that washed over you as it happened. You have to be able to identify facts from emotion, and understand that emotions are perfectly normal, but they shouldn't prevent you from living a full, happy life.

If you don't want to get dragged back to a place of deep hurt every time something or someone triggers your past traumas or hurts, then you have to examine how you've interpreted these events. Separating your emotional reactions from the facts relating to the events is necessary to change how caught up you get in them. Not getting lost in the sadness, trauma, or darkness of an event will depend on how capable you are of separating from the facts associated to it. It's about changing the way you react and what you are reacting to so that you stay in the present moment and prevent getting lost in what has already happened and cannot be changed. This is a vitally important tool in moving forward and letting the past truly stay in the past.

Once you've identified how your past holds you back, give yourself permission to let it all go. **Let it truly be passed**. Understand that what's done is done. No matter how horrible or terrifying your experiences have been, they are done. If you don't allow yourself to move on from them, if you keep dragging the weight of them with you every day and holding on to the fear or guilt or anger that you associate to them, then you're still there, in that moment, paralysed in time. You are living in the past. Living in the past prevents you from being present, and that is what the aim of my work is - to provide the tools for every one of you to live here and now with the blessings that you have been graced with.

CAPTURING MOMENTS

How much of your life do you remember? How much of your day do you remember? How much of what you've read thus far do you remember?

We are creatures of habit and once we have established what our habits are, we revisit them over and over again. Look at a typical day in your life: you wake up, shower, eat breakfast, go to work, get everything done that's on your to-do list for the day, come back home, eat, relax (hopefully), go to sleep, wake up the next morning, and do it all over again. Our habits and routines may change on the days we don't work, but even then, we have habits for days off as well. Basically, we zoom through our life, repeating the same moments over and over again without actually taking stock of any of them. In fact, the more we stay in our habits and routine, the more familiar we become with them and the less we remember from any given day because they all end up melting into one another, becoming one long-spanning, collective grouping of days and events.

Much of what we retain has to do with the effort we've put into it, and we are conditioned to retain and prioritize certain things over others based on a reward system. Through the educational system, the effort to study, memorize and absorb information gets rewarded by good grades and respect from our peers and family. Our performance at work gets rewarded by the compensation and benefits we receive from our employers, recognition from our peers and, hopefully, promotion. We willingly and gladly allow ourselves to be conditioned to do, say, and support things that we'd never otherwise align ourselves with for the sake of the payoff. When we do this, we end up focusing on the things that will lead us to the payoff, instead of drawing our attention to what really matters. Instead of focusing on whether or not we are loving and being loved, we focus on a paycheque. Instead of focusing on how we're treating others, we focus on how many hours we can bill. What we do in our daily lives by and large consists of going through the motions, with little conscious thought or incentive to pay attention to what we should be remembering when there's no payoff waiting for us. We let moments of truth, of hope, of import and of information pass us by as we zoom around in our circles, when what we should be doing is identifying and banking those moments as they occur.

Our mind's tendency is to wander - we begin by noticing something in our immediate environment, and that something reminds us of another time when something similar caught our attention. Who we were with, what we were wearing, what we had just eaten, how we were feeling, what the weather outside was like; the mind wanders briskly from the present moment to the past and the future in the blink of an eye. That blink of an eye then turns into minutes as the mind creates the non-linear path for the thoughts to wander down and suddenly we're gone. Out of the present, into the past or the future, but totally gone. The whole exercise in staying present is based in understanding the whirling nature of the mind and raising your awareness to **remain focused on what is right in front of you.** Once the focus is in place, the mind will naturally begin to wander once again and so the exercise extends itself to bringing your attention back every time you notice that it has wavered.

Another way to incorporate newness and stay connected to the present is to **capture moments**. Countless works of art deal with capturing moments. From paintings to sculptures to the most abstract and obscure of art installations, the artist's mind captures and immortalizes the fleeting for the rest of us to glance at, admire, and meditate on. These moments aren't simply cross-sections of the beauty bestowed on the artist or the admirer – they are cross-sections of truth. Truth that typically goes unnoticed as we rush around trapped in the confines of our own minds and thoughts, worries and dreams. In other words, the truth that we are immersed in and surrounded by becomes apparent when we are present, receptively observant to everything going on around us. The necessity to capture moments is rarely addressed, but nonetheless vital to our individual and collective well-being, because it is these moments and the appreciation of them that keeps our feet on the ground and our awareness in the now.

Capturing moments requires us to come back to the ease and simplicity of tapping into our senses. Try it: tune into the sounds around you. Look up from these words and take in what you see. Take note of what time of day it is and how the light illuminates where you are. Notice what smells and tastes are present right now. Notice how the clothes on your body feel, as well as how the air around your body feels. Notice all these things and acknowledge them. In doing so, you are tuning into the details of this moment, allowing them to imprint themselves deeper than they ordinarily would, thereby giving you more information to refer back to. You are helping memory come alive. If you've ever been stopped in your tracks by a smell, taste, sound, sensation or sight that yanked you back to the memory of another time and place, then you understand the power that the details in any given moment can have over us. Once again, it comes back to being present, and in this case, your senses are your tools in doing so.

Our society has started to clue into the necessity to capture moments, understanding how much of a gift freezing a moment in time actually is, but we seem to have lost our way in the process. Thanks to technology, we can whip out our phones in an instant to photograph, film, or record the events unfolding around us, which seems revolutionary when we think of how abstract the concept of a smart phone would have been just a decade or two ago. However, as with all things innovative and useful, the way we use it defines its impact on our world. Instead of snapping a shot here and there, taking the odd film footage of a memorable moment, we seem to be falling into the isolation that seeing our world through a camera lens brings. Check it out yourself: log onto any social media website and see how long it takes to find a photo someone has taken of the food they have on the plate in front of them. See how long it takes to find a photo someone has taken of themself. We have started to capture moments for the sake of public consumption instead of personal reference, allowing the validity of the moments we are blessed with to be determined by how many "Likes" they elicit. We have allowed what was supposed to bring us together and make our lives easier to draw us further away from each other, while encouraging us to find self-worth from external reinforcement and sources. So many shots depict way more than a militantly-styled plate of pasta or a self-portrait aching with self-importance. They show **solitude**. They show people on their own, so caught up in the false validity their picture will draw in as soon as it's shared on the internet that they haven't realized that the process of documenting that random moment has stolen another opportunity from them to connect with other people or the events in which they were involved. To not be on their own. To come back to the common experience we are all sharing, despite all the fussing over our tablets and phones.

> I used to take hundreds of photographs whilst on vacation, always in search of the flawless composition that would make for the best snaps to share with my family and friends upon my return. I would carry around the camera bag filled with lenses and accessories, constantly maintaining awareness on how I was holding the camera and if I was in danger of getting it stolen in a moment of distraction. When I wasn't doing that, I had one eye glued to the viewfinder, working to frame the image perfectly, get the right composition, and adjust the light ever-so-elegantly. The number of photos I take now is a fraction of what it used to be. As my vacations came to an end and I amassed thousands of images, I realized that I was growing tired of remembering my time away through the camera. Not only did I rarely look back on the photos, the moments where I shared them online or in the presence of friends and family became more and more rare. My trips abroad, my exposure to timeless works of art and scenic views,

> my get-togethers with friends, my moments of connection in classes and other group settings are now all filled with mental snapshots that I take, ones that when reflected back on, are more vivid in lighting, colour and composition than anything I could ever photograph.

The passion for what we appreciate in life, and the things that somehow reflect back to us how we see ourselves, need to constantly be identified and re-identified, stoked and fuelled. Our lives as children, and even adolescents, are spent capturing moments we've never experienced before and classifying them away for future reference... and then we get to a place where newness subsides, where we've seen it all and routine sets in, and we somehow allow this mediocrity to squash the promise of newness and the possibility of things to come. It shouldn't. Time seems to pass quicker as we get older because of it. Pay attention to the incredible events unfolding around you and assess their worth based on how they make *you* feel, not based on how they might be perceived or how they make others feel about you on social media. Acknowledge and be grateful for the people and opportunities in your life that you are blessed with. Take note of the truth and beauty in the details that typically go unnoticed. That truth is magnificence. It is timeless. It is light. It is everywhere, around and within us. It is in every single moment that we unconsciously let pass by. It is in the present moment. It may be disguised in the subtle and seemingly innocuous, but it's there nonetheless. If we miss it, it's because we weren't looking hard enough and, in doing so, we're settling for mediocrity. If we're allowing for mediocrity, then we are literally blocking out the light of a life steeped in promise and possibility. Capture as much of life as you can while connecting to what's in front of you, because in the end, that's where you will have found truth and fulfilment.

ENLIGHTENMENT

What does enlightenment mean to you? How much of your life do you spend seeking it? How much of what you seek do you already have control over?

When one studies and teaches yoga and meditation, many concepts get thrown around, but none moreso than the concept of **enlightenment**. Enlightenment through yoga and meditation is said to be the ultimate step towards connecting with the highest of energy sources, often referred to as God (see next chapter for more on the subject of God). It is referred to as achieving a state of peace, of bliss, of euphoric happiness, of nirvana. It is commonly believed that upon attaining enlightenment, one is released from the karmic cycle of birth, death and rebirth with the re-absorption of one's soul into pure consciousness. It's a hot topic among yogis and meditation practitioners. Students seeking enlightenment strive for years, decades, and sometimes lifetimes to reach that state of being. I've even been asked by students how long one needs to meditate or practice yoga before achieving it, and so to all who have asked me, and to all of you who are currently seeking real happiness and joy, I offer you this: **who's to say that enlightenment isn't already right in front of you?** Perhaps all that's needed is to allow for the shift in perspective and consciousness necessary to recognize the true moments of peace, clarity and beauty that are taking place right before your eyes.

Picture the last time you walked home from somewhere. Chances are you were surrounded by people. Chances are you were in overall good health and capable of making the journey free of pain or impediment. Chances are you ate a meal not long before, or were planning on eating not long after. Chances are you had things to do upon arriving home, and were coming from somewhere where you had gotten things done. Chances are you were able to smile at a passing thought or at the sight of something endearing or pleasing around you. Chances also are that despite all these luxuries, despite your freedom and good fortune, you totally missed moments of true enlightenment and connection because you were caught up in your thoughts, stuck in the past or projecting into the future. Chances are that in recognizing what was going on around you and how fortunate you were to be alive experiencing them, you could have connected to them in an enlightened fashion and lived enlightenment in that moment. Enlightenment, happiness, love, peace, truth – there are many names to identify it, but only one requirement: presence. You must be alert and awake in the present moment to be able to connect to what's taking place around you, and only then will you have the ability to connect to these moments of perfection. It all comes back to your presence of mind. Without it, you're gone, lost to everyone and everything you should be a part of, until you bring your attention back to the now.

Another way we are encouraged to find the connection that enlightenment brings is to stop focusing on the outcome of our efforts, to give ourselves selflessly, without attachment to the reward. This philosophy is based in the fact that, as mentioned in a previous chapter, if something benefits one person, it may be deemed as pleasant, but if it benefits more than one person, it's considered to be good or right. This begs us to pay attention to our actions and to identify when and why we do what we do, and who could possibly benefit from them.

Perhaps enlightenment isn't something that eludes us for our entire lives, but actually exists in the ability to stop accepting mediocrity and routine as the hand we've been dealt. Perhaps it exists in the ability to stop spending time and energy pursuing the abstract, and start letting our gaze focus on the perfection that exists right now, in full view, in this second. We are led to believe that we need to pursue enlightenment through a consistent and disciplined mindfulness practice, putting years of effort into it, and I generally ascribe to this belief. I also believe, however, that if we are capable of appreciating the simpler things, such as spending time with friends, sharing a good, heart-felt laugh with someone, seeing the beauty in our children, or simply feeling the sun shine down on our face, then we have access to moments of enlightenment. If we can sit in silence for any amount of time and feel true peace in the simplicity of the moment, then we have access to moments of enlightenment. If we can smile at a perfect stranger simply for the sake of spreading happiness, then we have access to moments of enlightenment. If we can perceive our actions as maintaining the integrity of our intentions, then we have access to moments of enlightenment. These are all different methods of attaining connection – to our friends, to energy, to people, places and things. It all comes down to being present enough to notice what's happening around us, and how we perceive it. Our intention will dictate what we choose to believe. It all comes back to what we consciously store our faith in and our ability to direct our attention towards it.

If we want enlightenment, if we want connection to a greater energy than what we're typically aligned with, if we want to live in a world where unity exists, if we want to see cohesiveness and togetherness instead of separation and segregation, then we have to set our intention to seek it out and choose to believe in whatever world view encompasses those things. Instead of choosing to view enlightenment as an ever-elusive dangling carrot, we can choose to actively seek out and recognize the magnificent in our immediate surroundings. We can make decisions that affect our day-to-day lives with a specific intention instead of simply letting ourselves be tossed around like a pawn. Have faith that perfect moments are not few and far between, it's simply our focus that eludes us. Focus in on who and what matters to you, and maintain that focus. Unwaveringly. With full confidence. It's up to us to create the lives we want for ourselves and shift our perspective so that we see things for what they are and not what we've imagined them to be. **We are the only ones standing in the way of that freedom.**

GOD

What does God mean to you? Do you turn to God on a regular basis or is your relationship with him/her/it something that gets revisited as a last resort when all else has failed? Do you blame God when things go wrong? Do all paths lead to God or are we the masters of our own existence?

Having brought up the concept of enlightenment, let's move on to God. There is a lot of God talk in yoga. It's something that I've never been entirely comfortable with, as I have grown to equate God with organized religion, something I have never ascribed to and find separates us more than it unites us. Having said that, I do believe in a higher energy and so when teaching, I tend to replace the word "god" with "peace", "light", "energy" or "love".

> I remember going for lunch with my mentor and friend Jennifer and her father the day after the Japanese earthquakes hit in 2011. We inevitably gravi-

tated to the subject of the massive devastation and subsequent tsunami that resulted from the quakes, and started talking about the footage we had seen to bring Jenn up to date, as she hadn't seen any of it. Once we had filled her in on just how devastating the images were, Jenn's father looked at me and asked, "So where was God then, huh?". I was caught so off-guard that I found myself completely speechless, unable to respond to Jenn's father, whose sly grin somehow embodied his lack of faith in God stemming from having grown up in the Nazi-occupied Netherlands. Thankfully, Jenn jumped in to save the day by switching the topic, but later on that evening I found myself really thinking about an appropriate answer to the question that Gerald had asked. I came up with a few morsels of insight, but decided to let it sit for a while to see what kind of clarity I could find by leaving it to steep.

Shortly after that incident, an employee working at a Lululemon Athletica location in Maryland was found murdered in the store. To address the incident, as well as the outpouring of grief that followed, Lululemon mobilized each of their stores by asking them to choose one of their yoga ambassadors to come and teach an in-store yoga class that would be dedicated to the family and memory of the girl who had been killed. The classes took place simultaneously around the world in all Lululemon locations, and I, as a Lululemon ambassador, was asked to come lead one such class. It was with the intention of turning a horrible incident into a catalyst for light that I finally found

> my answer to Jenn's father's question regarding God. I found myself channelling light to the employees who were hurt and weighed down by the tragedy that had affected their community. I found myself being "god-like" in my wanting to inspire those dealing with the after effects of what had happened, in wanting to communicate to them that they had the choice as to how they reacted to the events. They could remain grief-stricken, wounded and immobile, or they could see the tragedy as an opportunity to channel light and devote their time and energy to honour and help each other, as well as the family of the girl who had lost her life. I felt an immense responsibility to make sure everyone affected understood that their reaction could and should embody the energy we typically attribute to God. They could be "god-like" in how they dealt with the aftermath of the drama by bringing light into darkness, connection to those feeling isolated, compassion for those suffering. They could once again prove that despite there being a shockingly huge amount of hate in the world, there will always be more love to offset the negativity.

We turn to God when we need help, when things seem hopeless, and when horrible things occur. Conversely, when it seems like the natural order we live with on a daily basis goes topsy-turvy, we immediately question how God could have allowed such horrors to occur. I've done both in my own life with the untimely death of loved ones, when I simply could not make sense of the events unfolding around me, when I felt helpless and hopeless. What preparing the Lululemon class reminded me of was that God is in all things, not only the beautiful and non-threatening.

There are lessons to be learned from every event, and to diminish God's role to that of superhero to those in need shows how self-centered we can be as human beings. God is in every event, every moment, every being, including **us**. And because we have the spark of that consciousness and energy in each of us, we have the responsibility to be "god-like". At all times. In how we treat each other, in how we treat our environment (immediate and otherwise), and in how we react to events. We have a responsibility to bring **light** and **compassion** into moments of darkness and fear, to channel God's energy when it seems like we are most vulnerable and alone. I did my best to do this for the Lululemon class, and I continue to do so as often as possible: when friends are down and need a boost, when my loved ones lose their loved ones, when those I encounter seem incapable of breaking the surface of negativity that we can sometimes be inundated by. Forget about why things happen – focus on how we deal with them once they've happened.

Perhaps God's role in the act of any tragedy or disaster is secondary to the way that we humans react to the events. **Bad things happen to everyone.** Dwelling on these things robs us of the blessings that constantly present themselves. If you believe in God, perhaps you need to expand that belief to believe in yourself as the embodiment of all that is god-like. You already have the ability to access that energy and mind-set to show compassion, kindness and love to those around you. It's about understanding that role and connection. Perhaps horrors like those mentioned above serve as blessings in disguise, catalysts for the rest of us to tune into and infuse with our words, actions and intentions, conveying kindness, love, and light. Perhaps these events occur to show us how when the chips fall, all the inane squabbling and in-fighting we're all guilty of on a daily basis get relegated to the perimeter of our awareness, where they should have been all along, and the opportunity to step up as warriors of truth and solace presents itself. Perhaps God is not only in the **action**, but **in the reaction**. Perhaps. And perhaps not. Who's to say? I would never force my beliefs on anyone in the same way that I would never be receptive to someone trying to force theirs on me. It's up to each of us to decide what we believe in and how that sits with our world view. I think it's worth considering.

SOMETHING TO BELIEVE IN

What do you believe to be true? How strong are your core beliefs? Have they changed throughout the years, or have they recently been adopted?

If anything you've read up to this point is resonating with you, then you may already be re-examining what you have previously believed to be true to see if those beliefs still serve you. The best references for this process are *The Four Agreements* and *The Fifth Agreement* by Don Miguel Ruiz. Ruiz states that we are raised by people with certain belief systems, and because we are blank canvases with no other frame of reference, we adopt those beliefs as our own. He states that as we grow, we inevitably begin to examine whether those beliefs, or "agreements" to use his terminology, serve us as individuals and free thinkers. He then suggests that if at a certain point we find that something no longer serves us, we should break from that agreement and make a new one. His books offer five agreements that everyone, regardless of demographics or background, can practically apply to live a better life with clarity and peace. Ruiz's teachings give us the freedom to start choosing what we believe about society, about the world around us, and ultimately, about ourselves.

Our beliefs are more important than we think they are, because what we believe, we become. We create our vision of the world using the stories that we tell ourselves and the beliefs that stem from those stories. We rarely see things as they truly are. Instead, we see things through the filter created by the selfishness of our egos. We see things as we need to see them to feel good about ourselves and the world we live in. It's only through a real analysis of our beliefs that we can gauge whether or not what we personally believe to be true actually is on a more general scale.

With that said, as individuals, we need to find something in which we can put our faith. This entire work is a testament to what I believe to be true. Each one of us is here for a reason that is greater than the roles that are ascribed to us and that we ascribe to ourselves. We are alive, in this moment in time, going over this material together for a reason. That reason is greater than your role as a parent, as a sibling, as a child, as a friend, or whatever you do in your career. It is greater than your relationships, your insecurities, your stresses, or your bodies. When we get blindsided by the temporary, by the daily routine and the stresses that rise up within it, we stay cloaked behind the **veil of illusion** that prevents us from seeing the truth. That truth is this: we are here to examine why we are here, who we are, and how we are connected to each other and to the earth that continues to sustain us. That truth also states that beneath this world of change and separation is a deeper world of unchanging existence, and it is from there that we all stem. From a place of permanence, of unchanging energy and consciousness. We have the choice to believe that the waves of the ocean of existence are the sum total of what is real, or we can see the bigger picture and understand that the waves stem from an ocean, which in itself, is limitless and vast. In other words, we have the choice to see ourselves as independent individuals, or as a collective group of human beings all sharing common goals, dreams, hopes and fears. What you believe to be true will affect the choices you make in your life, and those choices will determine the degree of happiness and connection you feel towards others and your surroundings.

One of the greatest examples of this power to choose can be found in Jill Bolte Taylor's brilliant *My Stroke of Insight*. In it, she recounts the stroke she suffered in her brain's left hemisphere, and how she gauged the progress of what was happening by the gradual breakdown in her motor skills. Basically speaking, the left hemisphere of the brain is associated with language. It's analytical, using language and symbols attached to words to connect to the worlds around and within us. It's the list maker, rattling on throughout the day, and for all of you who lie awake in the middle of the night suffering from insomnia, going over what you got done the day before, the conversations you had, what's waiting for you when you wake up in the morning, why you can't sleep. The left brain continues to rattle on, depriving you of rest. The right hemisphere is usually associated with energy and colours, intuition and sensation. It's the area of the brain that gets triggered when you have a gut feeling about something, when the small hairs on the back of your neck stand on end, when you just feel that something isn't quite right.

Accessing the right brain is the gateway to accessing the truth about who you are, how you are feeling, and about what you truly believe. Real truth is pure being, without language or words to limit it. When you inherently know something to be true, it's known through feeling, through sensation, not through how you would describe it. Call it intuition, a gut feeling, a whisper, or a hunch. It is all of that and more - it is truth.

Accessing the left brain allows you to do your best using the language and words available to you to describe what feelings and sensations you have experienced through your time spent using the right brain. Ideally, we should all be striving for equal time spent using both the left and right hemispheres of the brain to live a balanced life. A balanced life would be one in which we don't over analyse and dissect every little detail, but understand that we need to have, at the very least, some semblance of organization so that our daily life runs smoothly. We don't drive ourselves crazy making lists and letting words whirl around in our minds non-stop, and we don't let ourselves get carried away with the world of sensations and emotions. There is a balance between the analysis and the simple act of being, without words or details, a simple sensation of being alive, of energy, of connection to the rest of the world. We find balance between the two, allowing them both to coexist in equal parts to remain grounded, but with full awareness of what we are doing, the decisions we are making, and how we are living.

During this trauma, Ms. Bolte Taylor's thoughts vacillated from the injured left brain's space of language and analysis as she tried to call for help during the ordeal, to the right brain's space of intuition, energy, colour and sensation. She went into the right brain and experienced pure energy, completely tapped into, and at one with the energy surrounding her – she even described the feeling as being one with the energy, not at all separate from it. She felt tuned into the magnificence of the energetic experience she was exposed to as her left brain was in the process of dealing with the stroke it was suffering. Her tale tells the story of what it was like to stay in one side of the brain and then to completely switch over into the other; to go from a place of logic and methodical execution of tasks to a place of pure sensation, pure energy, complete connection to everyone and everything. Experiencing what was happening from both points of view led her to understand that we have the ability to assess whether we spend all our time in either the highly analytical left-brain, or in the more energy-focused connection of the right brain so that we can find a balance between the two. She explains how we can choose to live life from a place of left-brained analysis, allowing the constant chatter to reduce us to listmakers and executors of what is on those lists, or we can choose to connect on a more energetic level to where we are and who we're with. We have the choice as to when and how we access the left brain (speaking, problem solving, writing, executing tasks, organizing) and when and how we access the right brain (meditating, listening to music, practicing yoga or any other mind-body practice). We always have the choice as to how we want to live and see the world, and that choice will inevitably determine what we believe to be true. If you want to live your life in a highly organized structure of logic, thinking and language, then you will "turn off" your right brain and access your left brain to do so. If you'd rather live your life by tapping into creativity, intuition, energy, colours and feeling, then you will "turn off" your left brain and access your right brain to do so. Moderation and balance between the two is the ultimate goal, allowing for a change in our habits and tendencies. Whatever you want to believe to be true will be, and so the concept that your view of the world and your place in it **is up to your own interpretation** using the two sides of the brain may prove to be revolutionary in helping you change the way you move forward through your life.

The only thing that separates you from being "enlightened" or "god-like" is doubt. If you doubt that it may not be possible to experience these things, then you will not experience them. If you doubt that you may never see life as a series of miracles, if you doubt that connection to your environment and the people in it is possible, if you doubt that energy can work through you, then none of these things will occur. The second you let your faith waver, then you are allowing yourself to get lost in "what if" and "but". The second you stop believing in something, you make the decision to allow yourself to believe in nothing. Your life will be what you want it to be. If you don't want a life of indecision and anxiety, then find your truth. Access your right brain and balance it out with your left. Sit with your feelings and sensations and be open to whatever arises. It is completely within your reach. You just have to understand that doubt will kill belief, and belief will motivate you to make the choices that will dictate how you live and how happy you are.

I'll tell you something else I believe: I believe in **messengers** - people whose mission it is to inspire and direct others towards truth and peace, using perception and certainty as the passageways of inspiration. I believe that the person standing in front of me in line at the grocery store has the potential to forever change the world, and I believe that after years of trying to find my way, I came to a place where I had no choice but to step up and accept that my time in this body needed to be spent in that role of being a messenger. I am now certain that I have stepped into my life's mission. What reinforces my certainty is the feedback I get from the people I counsel, teach and lecture to, encouraging them to pay attention to their natural abilities and gifts. I often find myself in front of a room of students, and the words come out of me with little or no effort. I feel like I'm simply the vessel for the teachings and information, and so my responsibility is to simply let it flow. What comes so naturally to me apparently doesn't for everyone else, and so I feel that obligation to guide people towards their own individual truths with that much more conviction. **Pay attention to what comes naturally to you** and believe in that. I know that I have had moments in my life when I assumed that if I had a natural talent or ability, it wasn't so special, that I was no different from anyone else and that it was probably the same for everyone. I now know better. Your mission has everything to do with your natural inclinations and abilities. Share them. It's why you're here.

Changing our lives requires changing how we perceive, interpret, and categorize everything our senses take in. If the beliefs you have held close to you throughout your life no longer serve you, let them go and find new ones. It's only normal in a world of continuous change and transformation to see our beliefs and opinions change. We have the luxury of being able to do it, but we resist taking advantage of it. Ask yourself why you hold certain beliefs and whether or not they serve you. If they don't, let them go and seek out new ones. What you believe will become. As within, so without.

SO WHAT?

So, despite our best intentions, despite knowing that we can decide what we want and understand what we need in any given moment, that we can act "god-like" when the occasion presents itself, and that we have the choice as to how to live our lives, why do we still look in the mirror and beat the crap out of the image reflected back at us?

Yes, we are constantly told how we should look, how we should dress, what we should drive, what we should eat, where we should travel, how much money we should be making, etc. We are encouraged to consume, to own, to horde. The more we buy into the media's messages of consumption, selfishness, and mediocrity, the more we find ourselves isolated and alienated from each other. The more we approve of and validate the digitally manipulated images of models posing in the latest must-haves, the more we are agreeing with and validating the standard thrown at us, which, in turn, galvanizes us to criticize, judge and harm ourselves when our reflection doesn't mirror that standard.

If we're so busy making sure our waists are the perfect size and that we fit the impossible standard set by the images on screen and print, we're **walking with our heads down**. We're completely internal. We're in the hypothetical. We have allowed ourselves to be distracted from reality. And instead of trying to make the world a better, more sustainable place for ourselves and the resources that allow us to exist, instead of focusing on how we're treating each other and making life better, we waste valuable time trying to make our own individual persons fit into some ridiculous image that amounts to nothing. We become reponsible for making ourselves feel unworthy of a standard that was never even based in reality to begin with. We become our own tormentor. Our ultimate goal should be to feel better about ourselves by letting go of how we think we should be and simply allowing ourselves be how we naturally are. This is not to say that we shouldn't give ourselves goals to better our physical body and overall health, but the second we create our own suffering, we revert back to walking with our heads down. We become our own enemy by turning away from truth, and away from making decisions that are beneficial in the long term.

I don't know about you, but my entire history of feeling good about myself is comprised of the moments when I made my own decisions, when I spoke my truth. That surge of confidence and contentment was the result of knowing I wasn't being manipulated into anything, but doing what I knew was the right thing for myself without any external influences factoring into the equation. When we allow ourselves to step up and be heard, seen and accounted for, that's when we start achieving a sense of fulfilment. The essence of what I'm getting at lies in **you becoming**

responsible for your own happiness, not letting it depend on what other people think of you. If you know that you are living your life on your own terms, then outside validation will be the by-product, not the motivation. With this understood, all the trivialities that we waste so much time on will disappear. If you have an extra 10 pounds to lose, **so what**? If you're not carrying around the latest smartphone, **who cares**? Really! Think about it... so what?

I'm a huge fan of the "so what?". My observations have shown me that every single thing that happens during a yoga practice is representative of something else I do in my daily goings-on. When I first started practicing more physical disciplines of yoga, I would lament the fact that I wasn't as flexible as some of the other students in the room, and in doing so, I reinforced the belief that it was ok to feel inferior because my forward bends had to be done with bent knees. Seriously? How is it that we get to a place where we allow something like bent knees to make us feel inferior and less-than?

The beauty of the physical yoga practice is that it's for everyone. Many believe that if you're not folding perfectly in a forward bend, if you can't get your leg over your shoulder, if you can't balance on your pinky finger, then you're not doing it properly. That is a trick, an illusion, the left brain kicking in to allow doubt and negativity to creep in. If you're not holding or moving towards the *Yoga Journal* moment, **who cares**? Really? **So what**? Are you still breathing consciously? Are you feeling some sort of benefit from your practice? If so, then that's all you need to know. Forget the rest. Forget trying to fit into the categories that someone else created. Take what serves you, try that which is foreign, and leave what doesn't agree with you.

When the concept of "so what?" presented itself to me, I adopted it in lightning-speed fashion, and I've felt a huge sense of lightness and relief ever since. Not carrying around the weight of the effort required to live up to all the standards that get thrown around has given me perspective and room for new experiences and opportunities that aren't tinged by negative thought patterns. Self-judgement wedges itself into our psyches early on in our lives, and we we try so desperately to fit in, to be accepted by others, to get positive reinforcement. That imprint lives on and goes deep, as demonstrated by the self-deprecating streak that trickled into my yoga practice. This was my experience. And when the "so what?" came along, the imprint started fading, and I found renewed confidence in myself and my abilities. I stopped questioning my decisions and choices, and I shifted my attention from how I felt I would be perceived by others to simply living my life according to what made me feel authentic and alive. I stopped micromanaging my yoga practice and feeling like I wasn't doing it properly simply because my practice didn't mirror that of the professional ballet dancers on the mats around me. That confidence eventually translated into how I was perceived through my teaching, because the way we see ourselves becomes how others see us. My actual tone and cadence of voice in the classes I was giving became stronger and more certain. My words flowed freer and more succinctly than they ever did, and students began to respond with greater attention to the information I was conveying to them. I now apply this attitude to so many areas of my life. I also present and offer it to my students and mentoring clients, and the effect of its simplicity is a marvel to behold. It's the easiest, most basic principle, but one that seems to be elusive to many.

I keep bringing up the yogic approach, but the yoga experience simply represents what happens in all other aspects of your life.

We let ourselves stand in our own way of attaining what we want. We paint ourselves out to be good or bad, deserving or unworthy, superior or inferior. By doing this, we attach to those labels and pigeon-hole ourselves into being that one thing. We then hold onto that label so enthusiastically and in doing so, prevent ourselves from growing and evolving because we stay attached to the past. We are more than that label. We are more than that one thing.

Understand that **nothing is ever one thing**: you don't have to live in a world where things are black or white, where your performance is either impeccable or absolutely worthless, where your reflection either mirrors what you see on magazine covers and is deemed acceptable, or doesn't and is deemed repulsive. If you respect and honour your body, yet still find fault with it, ask yourself why. Who cares if you don't fit some unrealistic mold? So what?

THE PURSUIT OF HAPPINESS

If I told you that I could give you everything you've ever wanted, what do you think your life would look like once I delivered on that promise? Down to the smallest detail, what you seek and covet would be yours, no matter how valuable, rare or financially out of reach you believed it to be - you'd have it all. How do you think your life would be?

Initially you'd probably be in heaven. You'd luxuriate in soaking up all the material possessions and comfort that you could wish for. Everything would be at your disposal. You'd short circuit with the insanity of it all, every sense heightened and on alert as you experience a major series of "firsts." After a while, however, I'd put my money on you growing bored with what you have. Regardless of how out-of-reach the things you'd been granted may have seemed before you acquired them, regardless of how complete you thought it would all make you feel, you'd grow bored.

Think about the last time you wanted something so badly that it became all consuming. We covet so many things – phones, cars, houses, money, people. The list is literally endless! I know that each of you reading this, at some point in the past, has had your heart set on something you didn't possess, and eventually got it. The elation of finally calling it your own was a definite high for you, a high that included feeling proud at getting what you wanted and increased self-worth by being validated by that exterior source. But as all highs play out, you eventually started to come down from that moment and your focus shifted to other objects of desire.

The process of identifying and chasing after that to which we attach usually proves to be an ongoing, never-ending one. What we don't already have can often be more attractive, so we constantly run after the latest dangling carrot until we catch it, devour it, and get hungry again. Like any addiction, we look to whatever it is we can possess or consume as that thing that will bring us the false sense of bliss that only true happiness can bring. We chase it and let everything else fall by the wayside in our pursuit. When we finally get it, we inevitably feel let down by the reality of the situation and the lack of intensity the experience had in store for us. So we assume the next time will be better, and we start all over again. This cycle is something every single one of us has experienced, and in many cases, continues to experience. It's an exhausting process: we incessantly expend mental and physical energy trying to possess, thinking that it will bring us the happiness that eludes us even in the most favourable of moments. What we haven't been told is that **it's not the attaining that brings satisfaction – it's what happens before the attaining that matters.**

When things come to us too easily, on some level we feel that there's a catch somewhere, that it's too good to be true. Handouts, in theory, are great, but when they actually materialize, they can end up feeling inauthentic or tainted; like charity or pity to some, laced with unease to others.

The fact of the matter is this: we feel happiness and self-esteem when we successfully barrel through obstacles and adversity in the pursuit of our goals. Overcoming the hurdles that we find ourselves facing throughout the pursuit brings about happiness. In other words, **our quest for happiness brings about happiness.** As we attempt to find truth and insight into who we are and why we're here, we feel like we are accomplishing something real, something relevant. We feel responsible for our own happiness and that in itself produces more happiness. The goal itself becomes secondary to what we discover about ourselves and the world around us.

I've asked my students the following question: if I gave you the perfect yoga practice, would you still do it? If nothing challenged you, if you never felt like you were accomplishing anything, no matter how important you may or may not have considered it to be, would you still feel the way you currently do about your life? About your job? About your marriage? About your health? About your relationships?

As far as I'm concerned, no one should be worrying about getting it versus not getting it, whatever "it" may be. **What we should be paying attention to is how we're getting it**, how we're moving towards it. The process of attainment far outweighs the quarry in terms of significance.

The end result may appear to be beautifully packaged and breathtakingly dazzling, but all of that fades. The struggles, the challenges, and the moments of accomplishment are what it's about. That is what makes us happy. Discovering things about ourselves can be dazzling and beautiful, and it's only in observing our behaviours and actions in the process, in *examining our life*, that we find these gifts. In the shift towards a new world view, we must learn to welcome challenges and adversity, because it's in dealing with and overcoming them that we find true feelings of happiness. Forget about the destination. Focus on the path that leads you to it.

CONSTANT CRAVING

Are you in any way, shape or form defined by the things that you buy? Has the craving to own and the acquisition of your material goods allowed you to create more stories about who you are and your place in the world?

One of the many stories we believe to be true is that we **own** things. We own the clothes we wear, the car we drive, the possessions that we have paid for. I am a homeowner. I have documents attesting to the fact that I own the property in which I live, sleep, eat and store my worldly possessions. My bank identifies me as the homeowner, as do my insurance company and the notary who worked with me during the purchase of the property. Regardless of how many people are convinced beyond the shadow of a doubt that I own my home, I can tell you that this information is entirely misleading and false. Yes, I have the legal documents and the insurance and the whole bit. However, if someone showed up on my doorstep with a gun pointed to my head demanding to take over my flat for whatever reason, I'd be out. I wouldn't even think twice. It would be theirs. I would no longer "own" or dwell in the property, I would have no claim over it, regardless of all the legalities and deeds. I would readily and gladly give up the illusion of claiming proprietarial rights over the space, and let it go.

The way I see it, I don't own anything, regardless of how many suited professionals speak to the contrary. I **manage** this home. I pay off what is owed to the financial institution with whom I am mortgaged and I manage the mortgaged property. This concept of managing what we think we own applies to more than just material objects. We manage our nutrition, our friendships, our relationships, our jobs, our family ties, our exercise, our wealth and our bodies. We are inherently managers, and the second that we understand that we really never have any right to claim possession on anything or anyone, a massive thing occurs – we stop feeling compelled to **consume**, to **possess**.

The concept of "mine" and "my" is a funny one. My boyfriend, my wife, that's mine, that was mine, etc. On the one hand, we would be straying from the commonly accepted vernacular to refer to our partner as "the one with whom I share my life", or to the car recently purchased as "the car I recently purchased." On the other hand, something happens through the appropriation associated to "my wife" or "my car." The usage of "my" establishes a real sense of ownership, espcially in the early days of a relationship. I have been in unstable relationships before in which I found myself incredibly insecure. I remember deliberately and enthusiastically using "my" to refer to my then-partner. I thought that in doing so my doubts would be assuaged, when in fact, it only gave me a false sense of security that later morphed into crippling hurt and disappointment when the relationship didn't work out the way I had hoped for. I'm in no way insinuating that we need to constantly censor the words "my" or "mine" from our language, but the fact remains that by using words that suggest one object or person belongs to another, an imbalance of power is created that keeps the selfishness of the ego sated and at bay. By claiming my ex-partner as "mine", I was able to kid myself into believing that my doubts were unfounded. It helped balance out my fears, which really only served to mask what was really going on.

When things don't go the way we hoped they would, when the reality of a situation proves to be way more challenging or problematic than we expected, we scramble to make things palatable and digestible for the selfishness of the ego. What the ego craves, it will fight for. The more we allow our discerning mind and able body to be at the mercy of that battle, the more we set ourselves up for disappointment. What we think we own, we will lose. What we know we manage, we will maintain until either we move on from it, or it ends in its own time frame.

One life lesson that I've understood from a very young age is that when things don't turn out the way I had envisioned, I was essentially dodging a bullet. I understood that instead of claiming ownership over the outcome of any given situation, I was better to manage it while confident that if things had gone as planned, I would have been worse off for it. To manage it meant to not let the ego's selfish streak get involved, therefore never having anything to defend, fight for, or mourn.

The ego attaches to what we think we own, and once it convinces us that we do own these things, we all of a sudden have something to defend. When we don't let the ego dictate what is right for us, we stop the pattern of measuring our worth by the objects and people that we claim ownership over. All of a sudden, we don't have anything to defend, because we don't claim possession over it. We manage how and what it may be, knowing that it will change from moment to moment. But we break from the selfishness of the ego, which, in itself, is a massive accomplishment and realization.

As I grow older, the less upset I get when I lose things, misplace them, or have them stolen from me. I'm a firm believer in the "easy come, easy go" mentality. I understand that nothing is forever and that as everything changes, so do the things I manage. Having this perspective ensures that I see things for what they are: simply things. Nothing to horde, nothing to defend blindly.

Know this: you own nothing. Being able to earn money that allows you to purchase what you'd like is a great thing because it shows you what you are capable of and allows you to live comfortably, but don't let yourself be fooled for a moment. You own nothing, and you own no one. You may have people who depend on you financially, but the moment you claim proprietorship over them, you allow the craving and the selfishness of the ego to control you. See all things in your immediate sphere as things you manage. Your body, your job, your material possessions, your relationships and friendships. You do your best to maintain and respect them, and you manage. They do not define who you are when you contemplate or acquire them, nor do they define who you are when you lose them. They are transient, as all things and beings are. When we are no longer tied down by the things we feel we have to defend, we are free.

TIME

How much of your life is spent doing things you don't want to do? How much of your time do you waste?

I'm not talking about the moments when you deliberately make yourself comfortable and detach from everything and everyone around you - I believe that everyone needs some escapism every now and again. I'm talking about staying in jobs that bore you or conflict with your ethics and morals. I'm talking about spending time with people who, for one reason or another, you'd rather not be with. I'm talking about staying in unhappy or unfulfilling relationships. I'm talking about doing what's expected of you when you're not authentically invested in that expectation.

One of the most important things I've learned thus far was conveyed to me by one of the co-founders of Jivamukti yoga, Sharon Gannon. While in Woodstock, New York, at a Jivamukti Immersion, Sharon lectured to the students who had come to the home she shares with David Life, the other co-founder. She spoke about many things, but the one thing that resonated the most with me dealt with the concept of time. Time is an incredibly obvious and important marker in our lives, especially when looking back at our experiences. The essence of Sharon's words were this: **don't do anything you don't want to do**. Hearing her say something like that re-inforced what I already knew, because I had lived my entire life up to that point only doing things that sat well with my soul, that I was happy to do and felt were an extension of who I was and who I wanted to be in the world.

> When I was in my early teens, with my parents desperate to get me out of the house over the summer, my father got me a job with the law firm where he was working. On my first day, I reported to my supervisor who took me into a room full of decades' worth of ledgers. My job was to re-copy the records in the ledgers in a more legible script. Unsure (and indifferent) as to whether or not my instantanteous aversion to the job was evident by my facial expression or body language, I told my supervisor I was going to visit the men's room. I proceeded to leave the room we were in, scurried over to where I had nonchanlantly laid my jacket, and made a run for it. I left the firm where my father worked (and where he had gone out on a limb to get me a job), and made my way back home. To where my mother was waiting. Incredulous. And livid. The fallout was pretty horrible, but nothing, in my opinion, could have been worse than spending one more minute in that room with the ledgers. At the expense of looking irresponsible and shaming my father, I was willing to take the fall.

I have always had a low tolerance for doing anything that didn't feel like a true extension of who I was. When I found post-secondary studies to be wasting my time (in that I didn't see the education I was getting being practically applied to any job I'd want to have), I would drop out. I'd immediately find a job, and work for a while, then go back to school studying another subject because it was what was expected of me and seemed like the easier road to travel. I was wrong. I kept leaving what didn't serve me, repeatedly having to justify my actions to my parents, but confident in my decision to pursue other avenues. From the friends I allied myself with to the clothes I wore, from the constant battle with my parents over my schooling to my choice of hobbies, I never did anything I didn't want to do. I still don't.

My mother once told me that one of her few regrets was that she and my father had raised my two brothers and myself to be harder on ourselves than was necessary or productive. After we discussed that for a bit, she asked me if I had any regrets, to which I replied, "None." The surprise she expressed at my lack of regrets prompted my own surprise at her reaction, but I am still that person – I have a finely-tuned internal barometer that I often refer to as my "bullshit meter", and when I feel it start to twinge, I know what I have to do. I have always been blatantly honest about how I'm willing or unwilling to spend my time, and I am so grateful to have always been so inclined, and here's why: what I have always known on a visceral level, and what Sharon Gannon verbalized to us during that Jivamukti yoga weekend, was that if we spend our time doing things we don't want to do, if we spend time in jobs we hate, if we spend time with people we'd rather not be with, then **we are deluding ourselves that our time isn't valuable**.

We treat our time in the body we've been blessed with as if it's a renewable resource, when in actuality, it is not. How often have you been asked to hang out with a friend who spends all their time with you complaining and lamenting their life? We all know that person: someone who is chronically negative, who has no intention of growing or improving their life. How often have you agreed to meet with them again, even after knowing that your time was going to be spent hearing them moan with an absolute disregard for what you may be going through? The excuse we give ourselves is that it'll only last an hour, that we'll be able to do what we really wanted to do afterwards, that it's easier to just go than to be honest and let the other person know we'd rather not be with them. We have all done this, and we have all had someone in our lives who was a taker – someone who takes our time, our energy, our money, our attention, while rarely ever giving us anything back in kind. When we kid ourselves into believing that we'll get that time back, we are tricking ourselves into believing that we've got all the time in the world. We don't. You don't. **Time is not a renewable resource.**

This is a call to the present moment. Make the most of your time. If you continue to devalue your time by doing what you'd rather not do, you're in for a rude awakening, and it won't be from me – it will come from that place of intuition. Chances are, you'll come to this epiphany once the best of your time has passed. Don't let that happen. You are the only person preventing yourself from making the most of your time.

WHAT YOU DON'T WANT

Do you get overwhelmed when you try to figure out what you really want for yourself? What past experiences and behaviours, in yourself and the people around you, have brought you frustration and suffering? Knowing what you know about life based on what you've already lived, would you do things differently given the opportunity?

We live in a society in which we are told what we want. Big business through advertising agencies and lobbies all work together to influence and sell to us. From what to buy to where to live, it's all fed to us in subtle (and not-so-subtle) ways. The success of these marketing campaigns is contingent on whether or not we rise to the bait and validate efforts to push products. If we do rise to the bait, lo and behold, we become willing participants in the game, duped into spending our money and energy on products and lifestyles we'd possibly never have chosen if left to our own devices.

Think about this: companies manufacturing electronic products continue to break revenue records by constantly updating their brands. Smartphones and tablets are ever-evolving commodities that once updated and re-released to the ravenous public, get purchased in lightning speed by the same people who bought the previous versions. Now think about this: if you bought a microwave oven, and the following year the same model was re-released with updated features, would you buy that as well? I would never describe myself as someone who would buy the same product over and over, but even I find myself drawn into the hype that those companies' PR machines create. It takes a moment of presence and reflection for me to remind myself that **I don't want to be someone who is constantly dissatisfied with what is in front of me**. I don't want to be hanging onto every new tech breakthrough with my wallet open, ready to be emptied.

How many of us, in the pursuit of our own goals and happiness, are able to sift through it all and identify **what we don't want**? Based on our lives and experiences thus far, we are all able to pinpoint certain scenarios and types of people that have brought us suffering or trouble in the past, and with that experience banked, we know what to avoid in the future. Choosing what we want in a world of endless possibilities can be paralyzing, so why not identify what avenues we'd rather bypass in the knowledge that they'll lead us to dead ends?

Consider the people in your life - do they bring you something unique and useful? Are they supportive and available to you when you need them? Or do you constantly feel like you have to chase them for their attention or time? Do they make you feel good about yourself or not?

What about your health? Do you consider yourself to be an active, energetic person? Or do you feel sluggish and tired? Do you eat consciously, fuelling the body with nutritional content that will allow you to physically perform at your maximum potential with full energy, mental clarity and focus? Or do you find comfort in food, eating senselessly when insecurities arise, consuming products that contribute to low energy and lethargy? Are your nutritional choices and portions appropriate for your daily expenditure of calories, or are you ingesting more calories than you need, thereby increasing weight gain and feeding those same insecurities that brought you to the food in the first place? Do you do some form of exercise for the improvement and maintenance of your physical health, or do you generally find yourself immobile, occasionally considering taking up a sport or joining a gym, but rarely with the intention to follow through?

What about your career? **Do you like what you do or are you proud of your ability to do it?** Liking what you do means truly enjoying the execution of tasks associated to your position. Being proud of your ability means feeling a rush of pride and contentment at realizing that you are more capable and competent than you thought you were, and having that rush of emotion propel you further on your professional journey. Just to be clear, there's no good or bad answer to this question. Your answer, however, will give you an indication of the shelf-life of your current job.

All these examples offer the opportunity for you to break down how you live your daily life and see if there are aspects of your reality that you don't want, either based on your past experiences or by simply paying attention to what emotions are conjured up as you think about them. The first step in changing a pattern or behaviour is being able to identify what isn't contributing to your ideal life, what doesn't serve you. If it makes your life better, it serves you. If it doesn't, it doesn't. The goal is to promote and prioritize the aspects of your life that serve you, and to alter or simply eliminate those that do not.

My experience has been exactly that, and I can truthfully say that I needed to close the door on my past career in order to make room for the blessings that my current projects continue to bring me. I felt like I was wasting my time, that I was destined for greater things than what I was doing. The biggest risk I took stemmed from knowing that I absolutely refused to continue on the path I was on, mainly because I was suffering mediocrity on a daily basis. I had absolutely no idea what I was going to do to support myself and maintain the quality of life I had at the time, but I was unwavering in the knowledge that I was no longer going to stay where I was. I knew that my career was not making me happy, and so I ended it in the knowledge that I would start something else on a path more appropriate to finding my true happiness. I didn't know what I would do, but I was damn sure of what I was not going to do. Eliminating what was draining me of happiness and energy allowed me to shift my focus to other options, and it was in that shift that I found my way.

What ultimately needs to be done is to identify what areas of your life need to be focused on, and to further identify what you'd like to see happen in those areas. Once you can put your thoughts down into words (I am a huge believer in writing these things down), and be able to see your goals clearly, then you need to start taking steps towards achieving what you'd like to achieve. Step by step. Nothing ever happens all at once – everything is a process, a series of steps, and so the first step you take towards your goal will be the hardest, as well as the most important. Its importance lies in the fact that once you get it done, you're onto the next step, retraining your brain to approach everything you do from a methodical place of smaller, sequential accomplishments that gradually bring about the changes you were aiming for.

Understand that choosing to eliminate that which does not serve you actually takes more guts and determination than to simply maintain the status quo. Clearing out the waste requires conviction, certainty, and a state of independence that, once allowed to come into being, will forever alter and solidify your ability to live *your* life the way *you* see fit. Eliminating what you know you don't want will leave you with options that will bring you to a better place – step by step, little by little.

YOU CAN'T GET THERE FROM HERE

How and where do you envision yourself in the future? If you could change your life for the better, what would you do? Where do you dream your ideal self existing and in what capacity? Now ask yourself: can I get there from here? Can the path you are currently on lead you to where you'd like to be? If not, what do you need to change to end up on that desired path?

My first yoga teacher, Joan Ruvinsky, once shared an expression that goes something like, "**You can't get there from here**." This piece of wisdom was apparently given to someone travelling by car on American soil trying to get overseas, but it obviously carries more weight than simple driving instructions. Sometimes our path brings us to a place where we feel stagnant, where it seems like the only way forward is to rethink and retrace the steps that have brought us to where we currently stand.

I've already mentioned the career change I made when I could no longer stand working in the corporate retail environment. I remember speaking to my friends and family around the time that I felt the major shift starting to happen, trying to figure out how to make room for that shift with the least amount of chaos. I asked them for tons of advice, posed countless questions, except for the most obvious one, **"How do I get to a place where my professional life is as satisfying as my personal life?"** If I had just been capable of properly verbalizing the question, I strongly suspect that the answer would have presented itself sooner than it did, but as all processes do, it had to play out in its own time. All I had to do was listen to my intuition telling me that despite not knowing where I was heading career-wise, I had to leave what was no longer serving me and have enough faith in myself and my place in the world to know that I would find my footing. I needed to let go of what was occupying the majority of my time and efforts to make room for something else. I needed to pay attention to the inherent talents and abilities I had been nurturing for my entire life, and try to apply them in different ways. Once the decision to let go of the familiar and leap into unkown territory was made, events unfolded, and the rest, as the saying goes, is history (or, rather, my story.)

Let's look at the space between where you want to be and where you are. Between what you want to speak and what ends up being spoken. Between who you want to surround yourself with and who you are currently surrounded by. Between what you want to devote your life's work to and where it's currently being directed. Between where you want to live and where you're living. Between how you're impacting the world and how you'd like to be impacting the world. It all comes back to asking yourself if you can reach your goal from where you are.

The space that lies between all these things contains one essential element that insidiously branches off into millions of tributaries: fear of **failure**, of not measuring up to what we think will make us look good in the eyes of others. The ego is afraid of never having enough, of never impressing enough, of never succeeding enough. If we want to take a step towards living clearly, visibly, wholly and fully, then we have to address the fact that fear is based in the selfishness of the ego. When we understand that the ego is ravenously trying to feed itself through our actions, deeds, and thoughts, then we can start identifying when the ego holds us back for fear of taking it on the chin. When we understand that the selfishness of the ego doesn't deserve any more of our energy, efforts, or attention, we start to live freely: free from suffering, free from failure, free from **fear**.

As seen earlier in this book, the fear that often dictates how and when we make decisions that end up guiding us through life, is a by-product of the fear of feeling separate. The root cause of most suffering can be traced back to feeling separate, apart from the rest of our families, peers, community and society. When we feel like a separation has occurred, regardless of whether it has been self-imposed or imposed by others, it triggers feelings of solitude and singularity, cutting us off from the norm. This sense of solitude often holds people back from pursuing their dreams, because the risk of failing in the eyes of others becomes too paralyzing. The fear of separation morphs into paralysis, keeping people from living fully. This separation is what Yogic scholars define as "Maya", often described as a veil of illusion, one that obscures our vision from seeing unity disguised as separation. What this means in plain old English is that instead of looking at everyone and everything as having common ties that bind us all together, we see separate faces and skin colors and incomes and languages and religious beliefs. We focus on the differences between us instead of the commonalities, simply because they're more obvious. Our work is to look beyond the obvious so that we can still focus on what we share, especially when we find ourselves feeling disconnected and on our own. Once we reconnect, we can overcome the ego-based fear that scares the hell out of us, and with that conquered, we can then narrow the gap between where we want to be and where we find ourselves. We can start to take the necessary steps away from where we find ourselves as we move towards where we want to be without letting doubt, lack of confidence and fear hold us back.

When a change needs to be made, when you realize that you can't get to where you want to be from where you currently find yourself, do whatever you can to tune out all that is external and listen to your intuition. Understand that when you actually start moving towards the life you want, things have a way of working out in your favor. If your intentions are honorable and you refuse to accept anything but achievement of your goals, things start coming to you: opportunities, help, information. That's how it worked out for me and for countless others. The only thing that separates those who are living a satisfying and fulfilling life from those who aren't is that the former overcame their fear of change, trusted their intuition and never gave up the fight to achieve exactly what they set out to. Understand this as well: the energy that you get back will be equal to, or greater than the energy that you invest. The rewards will always exceed the sacrifice. It is that simple.

HELP

When the chips fall and you get swept up by sadness or find yourself discouraged, are you capable of looking to the people in your life to help prop you back up and support you? Are you comfortable asking for help?

The topics mentioned thus far all deal with looking inwards, to our own patterns, behaviours, habits and tendencies, but one of the most important tools that we have in attaining our goals is outside of us: the community we find ourselves in. When identifying how we want to live and whether or not we need help getting there, how do we make room for our family and friends to be part of the process? At what point do we start speaking our intentions, and how do we ask for help?

Another character-building nugget of wisdom my wise grandmother conveyed to me was to **never be afraid to ask for what I wanted, because no one was going to do it for me**. As an eleven-year old boy, I interpreted her words as justification to ask for whatever material objects I found desireable at the time. Her words, however, took on a much greater significance when I found my 9-year relationship disintegrating in my late twenties.

> My partner and I were the couple that everyone thought was solid, and so when it all ended, I kept my mouth shut and opted to not bother anyone else with what I was going through. I really felt I would not only be disappointing everyone, but that dealing with my sadness would prove to be a burden to them. I felt like people would make comments like, "Well if you two can't make it, then there's no hope for the rest of us", which in hindsight, was ridiculously self-centred. When my friends and family eventually found out about the breakup, I was surprised by their reaction. They felt useless and hurt by the fact that I didn't turn to them when they could have provided a helping hand. By not asking for what I really wanted, by not falling back onto my closest friends and family when I needed help, I was treating them no differently than I would a random stranger.

I have seen this reluctance to reach out over and over again from almost everyone around me, especially when they need help getting through the rough patches. From seeing friends retreat from interacting for no apparent reason to finding out about health scares of family members, the reasoning behind their withdrawal is always the same: they didn't want to pass off the burden they were carrying onto others. In thinking about everyone else, they managed to convince themselves that to share their rough moment, to let their loved ones in during a moment of adversity, would end up causing everyone else pain, so the decision to carry the weight themselves felt like the right thing to do in that moment in time. In every case, they were wrong. In every case, they ended up preventing themselves from getting the support they so badly needed by assuming they were doing something good. All they needed to do was to reach out and ask for help from the people who loved and cared about them. It sounds insane, but everyone has done this at some point, including myself.

The people we are surrounded by are there for a reason, and they want to be of use in the same way that you want to be of help to the people you care about when they're in dire need of it. They want to be counted on and available for their loved ones, so when they find out that they've been excluded from a situation where they could have been immensely helpful, of course they're going to feel hurt.

Why do we think that we can only rely on people when times are good? We have to start becoming more interdependent, allowing the people around us to know that we need them and that we're there for them, for support and assistance, because the only way we will make it through life's challenges and pitfalls is **together**. If you look at the most successful people and what they've accomplished, each and every one of them can list a multitude of people without whom their successes could not have come to be. Ask for what you want. Ask for what you need. Use your voice. No one succeeds on their own, regardless of what they're doing. Everyone needs the security of a support network to rely on in pursuit of their goals and dreams. We all need to remember that no matter how strongly we may feel that we are individual waves, we are part of the same ocean and we have that ocean to depend and rely on when we need it.

CONCLUSION

All the subject matter in this book, all the questions, concepts and ideas, all boil down to this: **if you want to change the way you live, then it's time to change the way you think.** Your approach to everything you do needs to be examined, analysed, broken down with a certain degree of objectivity, as if you were reading about someone else's life, capable of separating fact from emotion.

If this book has found its way to you, it's hopefully already offered you tools to bring about the changes you'd like to see in your life. However, if you find yourself with too much to think about, too many concepts to consider and no clear idea of where to start, here are steps to follow to find clarity and create some sort of order out of all the subject matter:

1. Identify what needs from the Five Essential Needs are not being met to your satisfaction.

2. Seek out newness in your surroundings, especially in those surroundings that you are most familiar with, and take mental snapshots of the events you participate in and witness - the ones which move you, inspire you, or which you simply want to remember or refer back to.

3. Ask yourself how your ego may be limiting you from living, loving, communicating or feeling to your maximum potential. How do you feel inferior or superior to others, and is that feeling actually based in truth and fact, or have you been conditioned or influenced into believing its validity? What are you defending, and is it really necessary?

4. Determine what your core beliefs are. Do you believe in a higher energy, and if so, is that energy separate from who you are or are you connected to it? Are miracles and enlightenment concepts that you believe to be impossible, the lore of archaic texts and the superstitious, or do you believe them to be accessible with the right perspective? Do you believe that you can be happy by simply deciding to live a happy life? Do you think that life can simply be the outward manifestation of what you think it to be?

5. Understand that you are alive at this moment in time, surrounded by people and opportunities, for a reason that is greater than your job or any of the responsibilities that you have assumed. Identify what that reason is by paying attention to what your natural talents and inclinations are and then use them to bring something to the world that you can call your legacy, something that serves to reconnect and unite wherever and whomever possible. Do not be afraid to ask for help and remain focused on your goal.

6. See everything available to you as a non-renewable resource: your time, your body, your friendships and relationships. Identify how that dictates/defines your approach to life and what priorities grow in importance as a result.

7. Understand that every single experience is made up of an event enhanced by the emotions you associate with it. Moving past hurtful or traumatic moments involves objectively identifying and accepting the facts associated to them, with the emotions you attribute to them separate and disassociated. Once done, let it all go and give yourself the permission to let it be relegated to the past so that you can be free of the ties that have bound you to it for so long. Again, do not fear turning to the people around you for help.

8. Start to look for moments in your life, past and present, when you felt some sense of separation occur. Once identified, ask yourself what else you could have focused on to feel connection to someone, something or somewhere, and then use that as a reference for when the feeling of separation occurs again in your future. Stop buying into the illusion that we are all separate from each other and the world that supports and sustains us, and start looking at everything as shared. This sense of connection will change the rest of your life.

With whatever work you have planned for yourself, remember this fundamental truth: **it's way easier to fall back into familiarity and comfort than to undergo personal transformation**. It's far simpler to take the road more often travelled than to go out on a limb and explore new avenues. The easier path might feel more comfortable and safe, but personal growth, presence of mind, and the pursuit of happiness require confidence, determination, resilience, all combined with a real desire to change what is no longer serving you. If the way you've lived up to this point hasn't brought you to a place of happiness and contentment, then it's time to start exploring what else is waiting for you. It's time to dream big and incorporate greatness and, when necessary, take risks. Remember this: **no one who ever accomplished greatness did so without taking a risk**. Understand that you are the example for the world around you. People are watching you, and you are a teacher, even if you've never considered yourself to play that role. When people see others happy, motivated and enthused, they find themselves lifted up to the same level of happiness, motivation and enthusiasm. When people see others depressed and down, that too affects them. We learn from each other, and we mimic each other when we hear expressions or see mannerisms that resonate with us. We are all teaching each other, and it is through that teaching that cultural and societal changes start to manifest.

Many of you will encounter naysayers on your path to **truth**. This occurs because those who are unhappy want to see their unhappiness reflected back at them to make themselves feel better about the mediocrity that they've settled for in their life. When someone they know decides not to accept mediocrity or unhappiness, it challenges them (when it should inspire them) to do something about their own situation. Misery loves company, so if you encounter it in your attempts to find support, move on. There's no time to spend on people who want to keep you down. Understand the importance of the support network that exists around you and don't be afraid to rely on those who can be your support and cheer for you, even when you don't feel confident or able. **Be the example for others that your role models were for you**, and if you never had any, then be the example you wish you had been inspired by.

Take advantage of the time you have while you have it. If you want happiness and peace, then seek it out. Ask yourself the questions I've presented in this book, and see if they can somehow lead you to the present moment and allow you to let go of the stories you've created about who you are in the grand scheme of things. Learn to give yourself some slack! If you don't think yourself worthy of happiness, love, kindness and generosity, then how can you recognize and receive all those blessings when they materialize? **See yourself as others do**, even for a moment, and then understand that **the only person standing in your way of living a full life is you. The only thing standing in your way is fear**. And the same way you would tell your closest friends and family members to never let fear dictate what they should and should not do in this life, you should take that same advice. The choices you make and how you perceive them, free of fear, will determine your reality. They'll determine your happiness. With your spouse, with your friends, with your job, and all other aspects of your life. They'll determine how connected or disconnected you feel to the world around you, as well as to a higher energy. They'll determine how comfortable you are in your own skin. You have the choice how to live. You always have. Now it's time to realize it. Make the most of the possibilities available to you before they're gone.

APPENDIX: LEADERSHIP

Every page in this book has been written with intention: to help people heal, to help people acknowledge and identify what beliefs and stories they drag with them through life, to motivate people to make the most of their time, to encourage people to make changes that will only serve them to be more of everything they ever hoped they could be. An as-of-yet unwritten intention was also responsible for the creation of this book: to awaken people to the possibilities before them to become leaders, to help bring the state of their own lives, as well as that of others, to a more connected and positive place.

As demonstrated in this book, **suffering occurs when one is made to feel separate.** Separate from loved ones, from society, from what is considered to be "normal." Every time someone picks you out of the crowd to comment on anything that relates specifically to you, the threat of feeling separate appears. Not only can it come from external sources, it can also be self-imposed when we voluntarily step out of the crowd to take action or make our opinions and beliefs known, and even more so if we do it as teachers or leaders. The latter action poses a certain risk because to step into the spotlight is to open oneself up as a target. True leadership requires one to set a clear intention to reconnect people to each other and the world around them. We have always needed, and turned to, leaders to guide us through the murkier moments in life.

Each of us has the ability to be a leader. One doesn't have to control an entire geographic location to have the ability to positively influence others. From putting a meal down in front of our children to speaking to a stadium of people, the opportunity to step up and lead by example exists for each and every one of us. What we need to arm ourselves with is the intention of **bringing a sense of connection back to any and all who have felt it slip away.** Whether we counsel a bullied child to show them how their own sense of self is all they need to get past the bullies or whether we do our best to lead a country out of tyranny towards democracy and human rights, the underlying current of intention that infuses everything we do must be reinstating connection. Each time that focus is lost, we need to bring ourselves back to a moment when we felt that disconnect, and let the recollection of the moment re-focus us.

Once connection gets lost, doubt sets in, and doubt is a powerful navigator. It can prevent us from becoming who we're meant to be by instilling fear. Doubt steers us away from taking risks for the greater good and begs us to step back into the comfortable and familiar. It keeps us small, dissuading us from staying in the glare of the public eye and killing our momentum to do better in our own lives and the lives of others. And so this reflex of avoiding making ourselves vulnerable is a natural one, but it keeps us passive and prevents us from seeing our destinies as people of influence and leaders.

So, is taking a stand to bring people together worth the risk of inviting in all the potential negativity that contributes to our own separation? We are living in a time in which our world's population is growing at an alarming pace, and yet true leaders are few and far between. It seems like there are fewer people willing to step out of the crowds and put forth his or her candidature to help and guide others in the right direction.

Besides creating their own separateness by stepping out of the crowd, those who aspire to leadership positions also run the risk of losing sight of their goals, ultimately breeding separateness for others when the original intention was connection. Once the coveted position has been attained, leaders and other people of influence may find themselves at the mercy of their peers who helped get them there. Politicians, entertainers, and community leaders often have a clear vision of how they can better the world but, as no one reaches great positions without help from others, they end up falling prey to the agendas of the same people that elevated them to new heights. Maintaining the integrity of one's initial goal is absolutely essential in making a lasting impression, one that hopefully brings people together, as opposed to dividing them further.

Leaders, to greater or lesser degrees, need to understand something: it's one thing to get your foot in the door, but it's quite another to stay in the room. One can manage to get the job, the power, the title, and the bump in stature, but the only honourable way to lead is by example, one that is set over and over again by re-establishing connection among those who have lost it, to bring more peace, happiness, and overall well being to the world. We all have the ability to identify and recognize when our leaders and teachers make decisions that bring us further away from each other, further away from feeling part of a greater whole. We need to stay alert to this mismanagement of power and keep our leaders focused, but more importantly, we need to initiate this attentiveness in our own lives.

We are at a crucial time in history, when tradition and archaic laws and rules are no longer relevant or productive to the state of the world today. We are starving for charismatic men and women to step out of the shadows, ready and willing to assume the risk that doing so entails, in order to guide society forwards. Too few people are willing to suffer the fallout of speaking their minds in the hope of effecting positive change, but however few they may be, I know they exist, and I hope that some of them are reading this.

People learn through what they observe. Change occurs when others can see what the steps towards it look like. Masses will follow what looks achievable through the examples set by leaders, and so if you set your intention to spread connection and lead by example, others will soon do the same, eventually benefitting everyone. Each one of you is here, alive in this moment, reading these words, for a reason. **You are alive now to bring connection back to your immediate surroundings and to the world at large.**

Understand that to do something for the greater good requires sacrifice, but the rewards are manifold and will pour in with dedication and continued effort to succeed. Ask yourself how important it is for you to see positive changes take place in the world (around you or at large), and how much you're willing to give to see them happen. Forget about the repercussions of suffering the fallout of your own separation from what makes you feel safe, and trust that the connection you'll be bringing to others will come full circle and provide the stability and safety you seek. Are you willing to step up?